Microwave & More

SALLY W. SMITH
Editor

JANE HORN
Contributing Writer

**CHARLOTTE WALKER
& ASSOCIATES**
Recipe Consultants

**LINDA HINRICHS
CAROL KRAMER**
Designers

ED CAREY
Photographer

ROZ BAKER
*Photographic and
Food Stylist*

CALIFORNIA
CULINARY
ACADEMY

Ortho Books

Publisher
Robert L. Iacopi

Editorial Director
Min S. Yee

Managing Editors
Jim Beley
Anne Coolman
Susan Lammers
Michael D. Smith
Sally W. Smith

Production Director
Ernie S. Tasaki

Editors
Richard H. Bond
Alice E. Mace

System Manager
Christopher Banks

System Consultant
Mark Zielinski

Asst. System Managers
Linda Bouchard
William F. Yusavage

Photographic Director
Alan Copeland

Photographers
Laurie A. Black
Richard A. Christman

Asst. Production Manager
Darcie S. Furlan

Associate Editor
Jill Fox

Production Editors
Don Mosley
Anne Pederson

Chief Copy Editor
Rebecca Pepper

Photo Editors
Kate O'Keeffe
Pam Peirce

National Sales Manager
Charles H. Aydelotte

Sales Associate
Susan B. Boyle

Operations Assistant
Gail L. Davis

Administrative Assistant
Georgiann Wright

Address all inquiries to
Ortho Books
Chevron Chemical Company
Consumer Products Division
575 Market Street
San Francisco, CA 94105

Copyright © 1985
Chevron Chemical Company
All rights reserved under
international and Pan-American
copyright conventions.

First Printing in July, 1985

1 2 3 4 5 6 7 8 9
85 86 87 88 89 90

ISBN 0-89721-54-9

Library of Congress Catalog Card
Number 85-070885

Chevron Chemical Company
575 Market Street, San Francisco, CA 94105

Danielle Walker *(left)* is chairman of the board and founder of the California Culinary Academy. **Jane Horn**, a free-lance food editor and writer, has a bachelor's degree in home economics from Cornell University and a master's degree in communications from Stanford University. Her extensive experience in writing and editing on the subject of food includes articles for newspapers and magazines, a weekly newspaper column, and six cookbooks. **Charlotte Walker & Associates** is a network of specialists providing creative services in the food area, including food styling, recipe development and testing, publicity, and product demonstrations. The company is owned and directed by Charlotte Walker, a food writer, lecturer, and consultant. A graduate of Arizona State University with a degree in food and nutrition, Charlotte Walker has written three cookbooks and numerous magazine articles.

The California Culinary Academy: Among the forefront of American institutions leading the culinary renaissance in this country, the California Culinary Academy in San Francisco has gained a reputation as one of the most outstanding professional chef training schools in the world. With a teaching staff recruited from the best restaurants of western Europe, the California Culinary Academy educates students from around the world in the preparation of classical cuisine. The recipes in this book were created in consultation with the chefs of the California Culinary Academy.

Front Cover

A light entrée that's pretty enough to serve for company, Lime-Ginger Crab (see page 68) cooks in the microwave oven in about 3 minutes. Preparation can be speeded with the use of the food processor.

Title Page

Wild Rice and Mushroom Soup (see page 21) is one of the Appetizer and Light-Meal Soups found in the second chapter. Instructions are given for making it either on top of the stove or in the microwave oven, and it can be made ahead and reheated.

Back Cover

Upper Left: Leeks, carrots, potatoes, onions, garlic, and herbs are just some of the ingredients that go into a rich veal stock. This stock can later be used in a variety of ways for everything from soup to sauces.

Upper Right: Trout garnished with lemon and parsley are ready to enter the fish poacher, where they will be simmered in white wine and herbs.

Lower Left: Four Cornish game hens are arranged artfully on a platter with baby carrots and green beans. Among the lessons to be learned from professional chefs is that the way food is presented is just as important as how it tastes.

Lower Right: Rosettes of whipped cream are piped onto a cake with a pastry bag and an open-star tip. As a finishing touch, they add an elegant look to a chocolate cake.

C O N T E N T S

Microwave & More

TIMESAVER TECHNIQUES   **5**

The Timesaver Approach   6
Getting Organized   7
Nutrition and the Timesaver
Philosophy   9
Buying and Storing Fresh
Fruits and Vegetables   10
Utilizing Convenience
Appliances   11

**APPETIZERS, SOUPS &
SNACKS**   **17**

Appetizers   18
Appetizer and Light-Meal
Soups   20
Main-Meal Soups   28
Snacks   34
Soup and Sandwich Supper   36

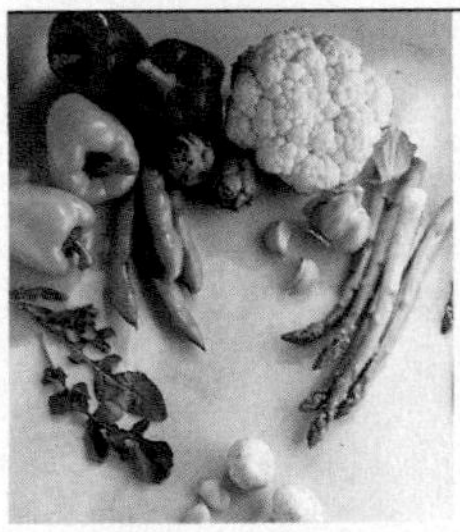

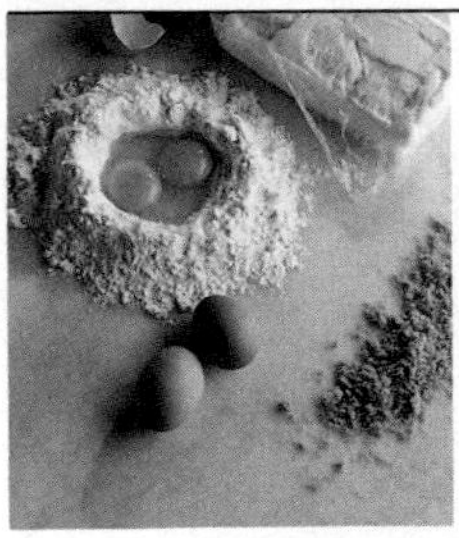

SHORTCUT BAKING   **39**

Microwave Makes It Easy   40
Frozen Batter Technique   43
Big Batches   49
Cookie-Jar Favorites, Faster   52
Shortcut Yeast Bread Baking
Techniques   54
Sleep-In Sunday Brunch   62

DINNER, QUICK & EASY   **65**

Microwaved Fish and
Shellfish   66
Top-of-the-Stove Suppers   70
From the Oven, Grill, and
Broiler   73
Make-Ahead Main Dishes   77
Dinner for a Winter Night   84

**VEGETABLES, SALADS &
SIDE DISHES**   **87**

Fresh From the Greengrocer   88
Microwaving Fresh
Vegetables   88
Luncheon and Supper
Salads   97
Side-Dish Salads   100
A Salad Buffet   104
Side Dishes   106

**FAST & FABULOUS
DESSERTS**   **109**

Chocolate Desserts   110
Fresh Fruit Desserts   114
Sauces and Toppings   118
Ice Creams, Sorbets, and
Frosty Desserts   121
Come for Dessert   124

Index   126
Metric Chart and
Acknowledgments   128

Fresh fruits and vegetables, flour and eggs, fresh fish, and good bread and cheese represent the basis of meals cooked the timesaver way.

Timesaver Techniques

This book offers recipes and techniques for making optimum use of the microwave—and more. It's based on the timesaver philosophy, an approach that blends kitchen management, menu planning, use of time-saving appliances, nutritional guidelines, and fresh ingredients to produce good food that doesn't require hours in the kitchen. This first chapter introduces the timesaver philosophy, including guidelines for buying and using convenience appliances. The remaining five chapters contain tasty recipes and timesaving techniques that make good meals easy for the busy cook.

A good example of time-saver cooking, Eliopulos Stew (see page 78) is a one-pot dish. Made of beef cubes simmered in a tomato-wine mixture seasoned with cinnamon, cumin, and cloves, then baked briefly to melt cubes of Muenster cheese scattered over the top, it uses only one casserole and needs a minimum of accompaniments.

THE TIMESAVER APPROACH

Time is something we all could use more of—for family and friends, for work, for recreation and leisure. How to wrest precious extra hours from an already full schedule is a dilemma we all share. The goal of the timesaver method is to give us back some of our day.

What does "timesaver" mean? It's an approach to cooking that gets good meals on the table quickly. How does it work? By simplifying what is prepared and by making the process of preparation more efficient. Menu planning, advance preparation, organized storage and work areas, and the use of such labor-saving appliances as the microwave oven, convection oven, food processor, blender, electric mixer, and freezer are key elements.

This approach parallels the new emphasis on diet, nutrition, and physical fitness. The trend is toward lighter meals with fewer courses. Our most creative professional chefs favor simple preparation of the best and freshest ingredients, and home cooks have followed their lead. Lengthy and complicated recipes are no longer the measure of quality cuisine.

Fresh foods also play an important role. To control calories, the focus is on nutrient-rich fresh fruits and vegetables, lean meats and poultry, and other complex carbohydrates—such as grains and cereals—that are satisfying, filling, and less fattening. Timesaver cooking techniques emphasize the natural goodness of fresh ingredients. Rich sauces are unnecessary if the food's own flavor and appeal are retained through proper cooking.

Cooking the timesaver way means that cooks needn't rely on processed foods, packaged mixes, and commercial frozen meals for convenience. It means time spent in the kitchen is productive, not filled with frustrations or wasted motion. And it means delicious home-cooked meals that don't take hours to prepare.

HOW TO COOK THE TIMESAVER WAY

"Keep it simple" is the underlying principle of timesaver cooking. It makes sense that if a recipe has fewer steps and uses less equipment, it will take less time to make.

Choose One-Course Meals

Soups, stews, skillet dinners, and other one-pot preparations are less demanding to put together and are quick to serve. Crusty bread and salad are often all that is needed to complete the menu.

Throughout the book, you will find dozens of tempting and delicious recipes for these easy meals. For many of them, instructions for microwave preparation are offered as well. For example, Hearty Black Bean Soup (see page 32), a thick and satisfying mixture, can be made completely in advance, refrigerated for one or two days, or frozen in serving-sized portions for up to one month. A microwave oven with a Defrost setting will thaw the frozen soup in 15 to 20 minutes. Sunday Night Seafood Stew (see page 32) is a perfect cap to a lazy weekend. The catch of the day is tossed into a broth seasoned with thyme, fennel, and bay leaf. Total preparation time, including cooking: 20 minutes. Sausage, Peppers, and Onions (page 70) uses one pan—a skillet—and is on the table in 15 minutes.

Luncheon and supper salads are easy on the cook and can often be pulled together from ingredients on hand. Mendocino Salad (see page 98), for instance, is designed to utilize leftover chicken or turkey. There's no cooking to be done, and the salad can be made early in the day and refrigerated until serving time.

Streamline Preparation

Simple meals mean not only fewer steps and ingredients, but less complicated cooking techniques as well. Grilling and broiling are popular and easy methods that produce juicy and flavorful meats, poultry, and fish. A dish such as Grilled Veal With Lemon and Herbs (see page 73) will please any palate and delight the busy cook. It's a snap to prepare—a minute just about does it—and under 400 calories per serving.

Foods steamed in parchment cook in their own juices; natural flavor

gets sealed in. Multiple portions can fit in one package, or each can have its own wrapper. There's little cleanup, and the aroma released when the paper is cut open is enticing. Many recipes can be adapted to cooking in parchment. See Citrus-Scented Fillets en Papillote (page 66) for one example of this method; it cooks in the microwave in 5 minutes.

Sautéing and stir-frying allow impressive meals to reach the table in 30 minutes or less. One such dish is quick Breast of Turkey with Mustard-Caper Sauce (see page 70).

Microwave cooking, in particular, gives new meaning to the word "fast." For instance, Amaretto Chocolate Sauce (see page 112), a velvet-smooth ice cream topping, can be prepared in the microwave oven in half the time it takes on top of the stove.

Keep Sauces Light and Easy

Properly cooked fresh foods don't need heavy sauces for a dramatic finish. Such sauces often only mask natural flavor, adding calories in the process. Seasoned butters make wonderful accompaniments to many foods. Use them as a topping for steamed vegetables, pasta, and grilled meats and fish, or for sautéing. They can be savory or sweet, and can be made in quantity and stored in the freezer for months.

Fruit sauces are naturally sweet toppings for desserts of all kinds. Use the freshest fruits in season and purée in the food processor or blender. These sauces also freeze well.

GETTING ORGANIZED

Organization sets the timesaver method in motion. If the week's menus are preselected, if meals are prepared partially or completely ahead, and if equipment, supplies, and ingredients are on hand when needed, the cook is serenely in control—of time and of what goes on the table. Planning saves dollars by minimizing waste and by helping you avoid the use of prepared foods, which often cost more than the fresh ingredients.

It takes time to save time. However, the rewards of a well-thought-out and efficient system of menu planning, marketing, food preparation, and assembly are well worth the initial effort needed to get it under way.

Setting Up a System

To start, pick a small block of time for which you'll make your plan—perhaps only three or four days. List every meal that needs to be prepared during this time, when it will be served, and for how many people. Allowing for the food preferences of family members, design menus that follow timesaver principles (see "Which Recipes Work Best?" below). Then prepare a shopping list from these menus, allowing some flexibility for seasonal specials and sales. Check staple items (see "Timesaver Pantry," page 9), and note what needs to be replaced. Try to do all your shopping in one day.

Which Recipes Work Best?

The elements of timesaver cooking are easy to recognize. Look for recipes in which many of the steps can be completed early in the day, the night before, or several days ahead, with the partially completed dish held in the refrigerator or freezer. Marinating, chopping and slicing, assembly of nonperishable ingredients, and partial cooking are

WHEN YOU RUN OUT

Even the most organized kitchen sometimes runs out of basic ingredients. The following is a list of simple substitutions for commonly used foods.

☐ For 1 whole egg: 2 egg yolks, for baking or thickening

☐ For 1 cup butter: ⅞ cup vegetable shortening or lard plus ½ teaspoon salt, for baking

☐ For 1 ounce unsweetened chocolate: 3 tablespoons cocoa plus 1 tablespoon butter or margarine

☐ For 1 cup buttermilk or sour milk: 1 cup whole milk plus 1 tablespoon vinegar or lemon juice or 1 cup whole milk plus 1¾ teaspoons cream of tartar

☐ For 1 cup cake flour: ⅞ cup all-purpose flour

☐ For 1 tablespoon flour: ½ tablespoon cornstarch or 1 tablespoon quick-cooking tapioca, for thickening

☐ For 1 pound fresh tomatoes, simmered and seasoned: 1 cup tomato sauce

☐ For 2 cups tomato sauce: ¾ cup tomato paste plus 1 cup water

☐ For ¼ cup tomato paste: ½ cup tomato sauce reduced to ¼ cup

common do-ahead tasks. Choose the less-complicated cooking methods, such as grilling, broiling, sautéing, steaming, stir-frying, and microwave cooking. Recipes that incorporate convenience appliances such as the microwave or convection oven, food processor, electric mixer, and blender are worth trying, as are dishes that can be frozen and reheated.

Adapting Recipes

You can convert favorite recipes to timesavers by following some basic guidelines:

☐ Do as much preparation and assembly ahead as possible.

☐ Substitute fresh or homemade for commercially prepared.

☐ Where it's appropriate and efficient, make use of labor-saving appliances, but be realistic (some small tasks are still done faster and with less cleanup by hand).

☐ Note often-used ingredients like grated cheese, chopped onion, chicken stock, tomato sauce; prepare these in quantity and freeze them in recipe-sized portions for ready use.

☐ Prepare recipes in double batches; freeze the extra batch.

☐ Simplify and streamline preparation: Substitute quick seasoned butters for complicated sauces (pages 75–76 and 96); in baking, use Big Batch homemade mixes (page 49), frozen batters and doughs (pages 43 and 57), quick-rise active yeast, and microwave rising (page 57).

Timesaver Preparation

Set aside time regularly for sessions of quantity cooking—in the evening, morning, and on weekends if you work or are out of the house during weekdays. Basics like stocks and sauces, and dishes such as casseroles,

soups, and stews, can be made in large amounts and refrigerated or frozen in meal- or recipe-sized portions.

Prepare for your cooking. Read recipes thoroughly. Note what ingredients are required and in what state—chopped, grated, sliced, cooked, raw. Have special equipment—pots, pans, appliances, knives, measuring cups and spoons—out and ready. Keep the workspace uncluttered, and clean up as you go.

Organizing the Workspace

How often food preparation comes to a halt for lack of a particular tool or ingredient! If the work and storage areas are organized to suit the cook, these frustrating delays can be avoided.

Keep track of which utensils and equipment you use most often, then store them so that you can get to them easily. Immediately replace any that are damaged or worn. Group all utensils for one job together—baking sheets and pans, sifters, pastry cutters, and rolling pin, for example. Handle ingredients in the same way. If you bake often, it makes sense to allot one shelf for flour, sugar, baking soda, baking powder, active dry yeast, cornstarch, and cocoa; put vinegars and oils together on another shelf. Once you've picked the right spot, always store equipment and food items in that same place for efficiency.

Make a master list of staples—pantry, refrigerator, and freezer. As much as possible, buy and store back-up items to reduce the risk of being caught short. Know the shelf life or storage period of these foods and use them within the recommended time limits. If you put older items in front, you'll use them first. Try to make a regular inventory of each storage area so that you know when you need to replace a staple.

NUTRITION AND THE TIMESAVER PHILOSOPHY

Timesaver methods not only give busy cooks control of the time devoted to meal preparation, they also allow control of the nutritional quality of food. Increasingly, we are being made aware of the significance of good nutrition. The interrelated issues of fitness, good health, disease prevention, weight control, and concern over food additives bring us back time and again to an emphasis on a carefully chosen diet. Fresh food simply prepared, the foundation of the timesaver approach, is also a key to good health.

Current nutritional guidelines recommend an eating plan composed of moderate amounts of a variety of foods, including plenty of nutrient- and fiber-rich fruits and vegetables and high-fiber breads, cereals, and pasta; moderate quantities of fish, poultry, and lean meats; and reduced consumption of fats, sugar, and sodium.

How does the timesaver approach support good nutrition? Since fresh ingredients at their peak of flavor, quality, and nutritive value usually need less preparation and shorter cooking times, timesaver cooks buy fruits and vegetables when they are plentiful and at their seasonal best (see Buying and Storage chart, page 10). The simple presentation of food cooked the timesaver way—with light seasoning and sauces—dovetails with the call for fewer fats, sodium, and calories. In addition, the recipes in this book emphasize dishes with good nutritional profiles: fish and shellfish, chicken, soup-and-salad meals, and fruit desserts—all easy to make.

The Cook Is in Control

The timesaver approach frees home cooks from dependence on commercially prepared and processed foods. Although these foods offer convenience, they often contain more sodium, sugar, fats, flavor enhancers, or preservatives than may be desirable. By following timesaver methods of planning, advance preparation, and use of labor-saving appliances, the cook can easily make the same foods at home—and tailor them to the tastes of family members at the same time.

When food is made from scratch, the cook, not the commercial food preparer, regulates what goes on the table. For example, regular canned chicken broth and commercial sauces are often high in sodium, but homemade chicken stock and pasta sauces can be prepared with little or no salt. It's as easy to use stock or sauce prepared in quantity and frozen in recipe-sized portions as it is to open a can or jar.

Storage and Freshness

Cooking with fresh foods is only timesaving and nutritious if you are familiar with proper storage techniques and know how long fresh food can be kept before it loses its nutritive values. Fresh food deteriorates quickly, even under optimum storage conditions. When quality is preserved through proper storage, the cook's job is much easier—less must be done to make the food appetizing, and waste is minimized. Food that looks good gets eaten.

Cooking to Maintain Quality

Even if food is carefully selected and properly handled when raw, nutrients, appearance, and flavor can still be lost through overcooking. Grilling, broiling, sautéing, stir-frying, steaming, and microwave cookery are relatively fast cooking methods that let the food's own flavor and natural appeal predominate.

Special Feature

TIMESAVER PANTRY

The following are staple foods that are used in the recipes in this book. Adapt the list to your particular needs, and inventory on a regular basis.

On the Shelf Flour, sugar, cornmeal, rice, dried pasta, herbs and spices, quick-rise and regular active dry yeast, vegetable and olive oils, wine vinegar, soy sauce, canned tomatoes, tomato paste, canned chicken broth, chocolate chips, unsweetened and sweetened baking chocolate, unsweetened cocoa, wine, liqueurs, bottled clam sauce, bottled chile salsa, onions, potatoes, fresh garlic.

In the Refrigerator Butter, milk, whipping cream, half-and-half, mayonnaise, mustard, fresh lemon juice, eggs.

In the Freezer Meat and poultry in serving-sized portions; make-ahead pasta sauces (see pages 80–83) and dessert sauces (see page 118), soups, stews, and casseroles; baked goods frozen as batter (see page 43); make-ahead Big Batch mixes (see page 49); seasoned butters (see pages 75–76 and 96); pasta; stock; butter; nuts; bread crumbs; grated Parmesan cheese.

BUYING AND STORING FRESH FRUITS AND VEGETABLES

Due to improved methods of storage and transportation, a wider selection of produce is in the market than ever before. For the same reason, many familiar fruits and vegetables are now available for longer seasons. The chart at right is a basic guide for when to purchase produce (note that foods are not always available at the same time in all areas) and how to store it. Flavor, appearance, and nutrient content are greatest when fruits and vegetables are bought at the peak of quality and in season and stored properly.

Proper refrigerator storage of fruits and vegetables assumes a temperature between 37° F and 40° F; produce should be in the crisper, in covered containers, or in plastic bags. Fruits should be ripe when chilled—they won't ripen in the refrigerator. Storage "at room temperature" means a cool room—60° F. Storage time will vary depending upon the variety of produce and its condition when purchased. The times given here are for best-quality produce and represent the period during which it will retain this quality; beyond these times, it will start to lose its prime condition, but it will still be edible. Do not store bruised or soft produce with those in perfect condition.

Type	Season	Storage
FRUITS		
Apples	September–March	Refrigerator; 1 week
Apricots	June–August	Refrigerator; 3–5 days
Bananas	All year	Room temperature;
		Fully ripe—1–2 days
		Green-tipped—3–5 days
Blackberries	June–August	Refrigerator; 1–2 days
Blueberries	June–August	Refrigerator; 3–5 days
Cherries	June–August	Refrigerator; 1–2 days
Cranberries	October–December	Refrigerator; 1 week
Figs	July–October	Refrigerator; 1–2 days
Grapefruit	All year; best late winter, early spring	Refrigerator; 1–2 weeks
Grapes	May–October	Refrigerator; 3–5 days
Kiwi fruit	All year	Refrigerator; 2–3 weeks
Mangoes	May–August	Refrigerator; 1–2 days
Nectarines	July–August	Refrigerator; 3–5 days
Oranges	All year	Room temperature; 1–2 days
		Refrigerator; 1–2 weeks
Peaches	June–September	Refrigerator; 3–5 days
Pears	July–October	Refrigerator; 3–5 days
Plums	June–August	Refrigerator; 3–5 days
Raspberries	June–July	Refrigerator; 1–2 days
Rhubarb	April–May	Refrigerator; 3–5 days
Strawberries	April–June	Refrigerator; 1–2 days
Watermelon	June–August	Refrigerator; 3–5 days
VEGETABLES		
Artichokes	All year; peak March–May	Refrigerator; 1–2 days
Asparagus	March–May	Refrigerator; 2–3 days
Beans, snap	July–October	Refrigerator; 1 week
Beets	All year; peak June–October	Refrigerator; 2 weeks†
Broccoli	All year; peak October–May	Refrigerator; 3–5 days
Brussels sprouts	October–December	Refrigerator; 3–5 days
Cabbage	All year	Refrigerator; 1–2 weeks
Carrots	All year	Refrigerator; 2 weeks†
Cauliflower	All year; peak September–January	Refrigerator; 1 week
Celery	All year	Refrigerator; 1 week
Corn	May–October	Refrigerator; 1–2 days‡
Eggplant	All year; peak July–September	Cool room temperature; 1–2 days
Lettuce	All year	Refrigerator; 1 week
Mushrooms	All year	Refrigerator; 1–2 days
Okra	July–October	Refrigerator; 3–5 days
Onions (green)	All year	Refrigerator; 3–5 days
Onions (red, white, yellow)	All year	Dry room temperature with good air circulation; 2–3 months
Parsnips	All year; peak November–March	Refrigerator; 2 weeks
Peas, green	March–May; September–November	Refrigerator; 3–5 days (in the pod, uncovered)
Peppers	All year; peak June–November	Refrigerator; 1 week
Potatoes*	All year	Cool (45°–50° F), dark, dry, well-ventilated place; 1–2 months
Spinach	All year; peak December–May	Refrigerator; 3–5 days
Summer squash	All year (not all varieties); peak June–September	Refrigerator; 3–5 days
Tomatoes	All year; peak May–September	Room temperature away from direct sunlight; 2–3 days
Winter squash*	All year (some varieties); peak August–December	Cool room temperature; 1–2 months

* If you're unable to store at recommended temperature, buy only enough for one week's use and keep in cool, dark place.   † Remove tops.   ‡ Unhusked and uncovered.

UTILIZING CONVENIENCE APPLIANCES

A fundamental principle behind the recipes in this book is the use of appliances whenever they can save time without a reduction in the quality of cooking. To be worth the cost, the machines must do the jobs faster and more efficiently (including the time involved in cleanup) than they can be done by hand. Do you need all the machines described in this section? The factors to consider include how you cook, in what quantity, your budget, and how much counter and storage space is available for equipment. Then you can decide if it makes sense for you to have a number of appliances that perform very specific tasks, or if one or two will do the trick.

MICROWAVE OVEN

The microwave oven is fast becoming America's most popular major appliance, according to manufacturers' sales figures. At least one third of all homes in this country have one, and the number is growing.

Microwave cookery is quick, cool, and clean. Many foods cook in one fourth the time and with less energy than in a conventional oven or on a surface cooking unit. The microwave oven puts out no heat—only the food gets hot—so the kitchen and the cook stay comfortably cool. Cleanup and maintenance are easy: Because food doesn't bake onto the dish or the oven walls, equipment and utensils wash clean with a sponge and soapy water, and the oven requires only an occasional wipe with a damp cloth to remove spills and spatters. Microwave ovens plug into regular household current and are sold in a range of sizes to fit into almost any space, so most kitchens can easily accommodate one.

How Does It Work?

Microwaves are short, high-frequency radio waves. They are reflected by metal, but pass through glass, paper, ceramic, and some plastics, and are attracted to the moisture, fat, and sugar content of food.

A magnetron tube inside each microwave oven converts electricity into high-frequency energy—the microwaves—and transmits the microwaves into the oven cavity. Because of their special properties, microwaves bounce off the metallic oven walls and are absorbed by food. Inside the food, microwaves cause water molecules to vibrate very rapidly and rub against one another and adjoining molecules. This friction produces heat, which cooks the food from the outside in.

When to Use a Microwave Oven

The foods that do best in a microwave oven are those that in a conventional oven are cooked with moist heat. Because cooking time is brief and little water is used, vegetables retain vivid color, crisp texture, and valuable nutrients; fish poaches juicy, firm, and delicately flavored in minutes; stews, casseroles, and sauced foods usually cook in less time and with minimal cleanup.

Microwave ovens are the ideal complement to the home freezer. With defrost capability, a microwave oven can thaw a frozen dish and then heat the food to serving temperature. Reheated foods stay fresh, with no warmed-over taste.

Other Factors to Consider

The microwave oven is a kitchen miracle worker for many tasks, but it isn't perfect. It will not brown most food or produce a crisp crust, which limits its appropriateness for cooking meats or baking. Those baked goods that do not need a browned top—for instance, a sheet cake that will be frosted—may still not be as good when baked in a microwave oven as they would be when baked conventionally; the microwave performs best with rich batter baked in a round pan. Some dishes cook unevenly (this may be less of a problem with newer models). Bringing a liquid to a boil can take every bit as long in a microwave as on top of the stove, and cooking in large quantities can also negate the time savings. It's also quite easy—because of unfamiliarity with either the oven or the recipe—to overcook foods. And it can be difficult to feel comfortable with a new cooking technology.

A microwave cooking class is a good way to learn what the oven does best and how this appliance can be integrated with your individual cooking style.

Which Oven for You?

Today, microwave ovens offer many options. They come full-size, mid-size, and compact; portable or built-in; paired with a full-size conventional oven, combined with a conventional oven in one unit, or combined with a convection oven in one unit.

Although for space reasons you may lean toward one of the combination units, for optimum benefits from the microwave, it's probably best to buy a single-purpose oven. If counter space is at a premium in your kitchen, lightweight models can be hung under a cabinet, or an oven can be set into existing cabinet space. Keep in mind, however, that the smaller models are usually less powerful—which means slower cooking—and will hold less. This won't matter for one or two persons, but it will make a difference when you are cooking for four or more.

If you often cook with a particular dish, bring it along when you're shopping, to find an oven that can hold it. If you can use what you've already got at home, that's one less adjustment you will have to make when you switch to microwave cooking.

Look for an oven with at least four power levels—High, Medium, and Low, plus Defrost. Some ovens have just one setting that is basically useful only for reheating; other models have as many as ten settings. Each setting corresponds to a percentage of power. Generally, High is 100% power, Medium is 50% power, and so on—but not always; be sure to check manufacturer's instructions to learn what percentage your oven is operating with at each setting. Be-cause the settings have different meanings for different ovens, the recipes in this book specify settings in percentages.

Most full-size ovens feature 600 to 720 watts, and most recipes—including those in this book—are written for ovens of this wattage. Some smaller ovens have less wattage, and therefore less power, at each setting. Recipes must be adjusted accordingly. Manufacturers' directions will guide you in making this adjustment; see also "Microwave Cooking" and "Adapting Recipes for the Microwave" on the facing page.

There are a number of other options among which you can choose. For roasts and for judging the internal temperature of a mass of food, including liquids, consider an oven with a temperature probe. Ovens with electronic programming can be set to heat to a predetermined temperature when used with a probe. Another variable is the kind of control—you can choose a dial or a touch panel control. Dial control ovens are usually less expensive, but give less precise settings. Touch panels are more accurate for smaller amounts of time—and with microwave cooking, seconds can make a difference.

Other features include racks; turntables (developed to correct uneven cooking, they limit the size of the cooking dish to one that fits the turntable); clocks; and electronic programming, which permits multistage cooking—defrost/reheat, cook/hold, delay/cook/hold, for example. The features you need will depend on how you intend to use your oven. Some stores will allow you to exchange your oven for another model within a certain period of time if you decide that your first choice wasn't the right one.

Utensils and Equipment

Before buying special cookware for use in your microwave, inventory what you have on hand. Most kitchens are already well stocked with microwave-safe cookware. To be microwave safe, cookware must be of a type that will not get hot in the oven, except where it comes in contact with hot food. (To test a dish for microwave use, place it in the oven along with a 1-cup measure filled with water. Microwave on 100% power for 1 minute. If the water is warm and the dish cool, the dish is microwave safe.)

Among the items used for conventional cooking that you can also use in the microwave are heat-resistant glass baking dishes, pie plates, mixing bowls, measuring and custard cups, and ceramic serving dishes. Avoid metal and metal-trimmed cookware. Metal reflects microwaves; using it will give you uneven cooking, and could cause arcing—sparks that may damage the oven. The one exception to the no-metal-in-the-microwave rule is aluminum foil, which is often used to shield fast-cooking areas of a dish—such as poultry wings and breast, or the corners of baked goods—to prevent overcooking.

Other cooking materials that you can use in the microwave include paper plates, paper napkins, paper towels, waxed paper, heavy plastic wrap, ovenproof cooking bags, and plastic-coated paper containers. The fact that you can cook with these disposable materials is another of the microwave's advantages; cleanup can be as simple as throwing away the cooking container.

Once you've used the microwave a bit, you may want to consider getting some special equipment. The possibilities include: a microwave thermometer (used like a probe to gauge internal temperature); a roasting rack; a scale (microwave cooking is often calculated in minutes-per-pound); and a browning dish (which essentially sears color onto meats and poultry).

Microwave Cooking

As with most cooking, experience is the best teacher for using the microwave. The sooner you incorporate the microwave oven into your daily routine, the more quickly you will gain confidence and realize its full potential as a timesaver appliance.

Microwave cooking is based on time, not heat. To avoid overcooking, keep in mind the following variables:

☐ Shape of food: Thin pieces cook faster.

☐ Temperature at start of cooking: Chilled foods take longer to heat.

☐ Amount of food: When you double the quantity, the cooking time is nearly doubled.

☐ Composition of food: Low-moisture, high-fat, and high-sugar content foods cook faster.

☐ Density of food: Porous foods cook faster.

☐ Oven power: Ovens with higher wattage ratings cook faster at each power setting.

☐ Carryover cooking: Food continues to heat internally even after cooking has stopped, so always undercook to avoid drying out the food.

Because of all these variables, no recipe can give the exact instructions you will need for optimum results. Recipes should be considered guides to successful microwave cooking; some experimentation with your particular oven, as well as careful checking as dishes cook, will be required.

Uneven cooking—a major problem—is the result of uneven microwave penetration. Microwaves are attracted to corners and edges. In newer models, stirrer fans in the oven wall help distribute the energy in a better pattern. Turntables serve the same purpose. To assure even heating, put the quickest-cooking area of the food in the center; arrange food in a circular pattern or use round dishes, if possible; rotate food during cooking time; stir food to bring cooked edges in and still-raw center portions out.

In microwave cooking, food is often covered to control moisture loss or to prevent spattering. If a recipe calls for a cover, use a tight-fitting lid or plastic wrap. For protection against spattering, use waxed paper, a paper towel, or a paper napkin. With high temperatures, pierce plastic wrap or lift a corner to allow the steam to escape.

Adapting Recipes for the Microwave

Manufacturers' instruction books will give guidelines for converting recipes for conventional ovens to the microwave. As a rule of thumb, you'll find that you will need to decrease time by as much as 75 percent and liquids by up to 50 percent. Time and power setting can be estimated by comparing the recipe to a similar one already written for the microwave oven.

CONVECTION OVEN

A favorite with bakers for its even browning and fast cooking, the convection oven cooks up to one-third faster than conventional ovens and at lower temperatures for many foods. As a result, these ovens save energy as well as time. No special utensils are needed and, except for broiling, preheating is not required. Most are portable, designed to sit on a counter or recess into cabinet space.

A fan in the convection oven cavity blows air over the heating element and keeps the hot air constantly circulating. Thus, these ovens are ideal for foods requiring hot, dry, circulating air—roasted and broiled meats and poultry, fish, and baked goods of all kinds.

If you bake frequently or enjoy roasted and broiled meals you will appreciate this oven's unique capabilities. Options include dial or electronic touch controls, temperature probe, multistage programming, dehydrator racks, and continuous cleaning.

Follow the manufacturer's recommendations when determining time and temperature. As a general rule, to adapt a recipe written for roasting in a conventional oven, decrease roasting time by 30 percent and keep the temperature the same. To bake a casserole, you should be able to keep heat and time about the same as in a conventional oven. For leavened baked goods, decrease temperature by 50° F to 75° F; time may be slightly less.

FREEZER

A well-stocked chest or upright freezer plays an important role in time-saver cooking. Whole meals or components of many dishes can be prepared in multiple batches and frozen for later use, with little nutritional change. If you expect to do any serious freezing, you'll need a freezer rather than a freezing compartment of a refrigerator. A freezer's generous capacity allows the cook to stock up during sales and when favorite foods are in season. Home freezers reach and maintain the optimum temperature—0° F—needed to preserve food quality better than refrigerator-freezer combinations. Fluctuations in temperature, common in the combination appliances, have an adverse effect on frozen food; with every 10° F above zero, storage life is cut by up to half.

When selecting a freezer, size should be the first consideration. Allow 5 to 6 cubic feet per family member. Buy the size you'll use to best advantage, keeping in mind that freezers should always be at least two-thirds full for maximum efficiency.

Chest or upright? Of the two, chest freezers are generally cheaper to buy and operate. Less cold air escapes the top-opening lid, and therefore less energy is needed to keep the temperature constant. Chest

freezers hold more than uprights, need defrosting less often, and defrost more quickly as well. They need more floor space, however, and food is more difficult to arrange and harder to retrieve, although most chest models now come with lift-out or sliding baskets that help to alleviate this problem.

Upright models take up less space and offer an automatic defrost option. Easy-to-reach shelves and door storage make the upright increasingly popular, although it is less energy efficient.

To make the best use of your freezer, be sure foods are sealed airtight with wrapping material or containers designed for freezing. Use materials that are airtight, vapor-proof, and moistureproof. On the market are flexible plastic food-storage bags (use only those labeled suitable for freezing), heavy-duty aluminum foil, plastic freezer wrap, and coated freezer paper. Rigid containers include glass freezer jars, ovenproof casseroles, plastic freezer containers, aluminum foil containers, wax-coated cardboard cartons, tin cans, and ice cube trays or muffin tins.

Food loses quality if stored too long or at improper temperatures (although it is still safe to eat). Keep an inventory of the foods you have in storage so that you'll know what's on hand and how long it has been there. Label each item with contents, date, weight, and number of servings. Periodically check the freezer temperature to be sure that it is at 0° F or a little below.

ELECTRIC MIXER

There is no better way to whip cream, beat egg whites, and mix up light, airy cake batters than with an electric mixer. There are two kinds of mixers: portable and stand. The portable or hand-held version is the simplest; the cook holds the machine with the beaters inserted into a bowl and controls the movement of the mixer.

Portable mixers differ from one another primarily in power and speed settings. The higher-quality ones may also come with dough hooks for kneading, and a few attach to a separate base, allowing the mixer to function as both portable and stand. Hand-held mixers are lightweight, easy to store, and can be moved around the kitchen. On the other hand, the cook can't do other tasks while holding the mixer, and holding it can be tiring. Some portable mixers lose strength when working on stiff doughs.

Stand mixers range from light to heavy duty. Electronic controls help maintain speed as the mixture gets heavier; some also have a timer. Bowl capacity is usually around 4 quarts, but other sizes are available. Some have a flat, open beater, plus a whisk for whipping, and a dough hook. Among the attachments available are food grinders, juicers, slicer/shredders, sausage stuffers, pasta makers, and grain grinders.

Serious bakers are advised to buy a quality, heavy-duty stand mixer. Otherwise, most mixing can be done with a good portable.

FOOD PROCESSOR

The multifunction food processor makes quick work out of many tedious and time-consuming culinary chores. With one machine, the cook can chop, slice, shred, mix, and purée almost instantaneously. The more powerful processors have the muscle to knead heavy bread dough with little effort. Many cooks consider this extremely versatile machine their most valuable kitchen appliance.

The food processor is composed of a motor-driven shaft, a work bowl that fits over the shaft, and various blades and disks that attach to the shaft inside the work bowl, rotating at high speed when the machine is on. Food is either placed directly in the bowl or fed in through a tube on the bowl's cover.

Food processors are most efficient when used for several consecutive tasks. It's often faster and easier to do a single small job by hand—chop one clove of garlic or a tablespoon of parsley—than it is to set up the machine and have to face cleanup afterwards. On the other hand, a recipe that calls for a variety of chopped vegetables—say, to be sautéed and then puréed for a soup—is perfect for the food processor.

Models vary in capacity and power from the very compact to machines intended for cooks who prepare food on a large scale. Which to buy depends on how often you will use the machine and the amount of food you will need to prepare at one time. A larger work bowl will obviously hold more—some as much as 16 cups of chopped or shredded food, or up to 7 cups of liquid. These maximum-capacity machines need a powerful motor for peak performance and are thus highest in price. Unless it has a special whisk or beater attachment, a food processor will not whip egg whites or cream to maximum volume, nor will it make acceptable mashed potatoes, all of which a mixer can do. It also cannot grind coffee beans, grains, or hard spices, as a blender can.

Standard with most processors are a multipurpose steel blade for blending, mixing, and puréeing; a plastic dough blade; a slicing disk; and a shredding disk. Common options include an expanded or whole-bowl feed tube that will accommodate larger items such as an entire tomato or onion, or several at once; a range of slicers and shredders, including a french fry cutter; a whisk or beaters for beating egg whites and whipping cream; a pasta-making attachment; and a citrus juicer.

The machine is so fast that control of its speed is critical to obtaining a quality final product. Proper technique makes the difference between finely ground nuts and nut butter, or chopped onions and onion purée. Many models have a pulse action that turns the motor on and off in bursts, letting the cook monitor the processing more accurately.

BLENDER

The blender is often compared with the food processor, and often suffers in the comparison. But it has its virtues. The blender purées, chops, and grates; makes silken sauces and mayonnaise; and mixes the best drinks. Its tall, narrow container is better designed for some jobs than the food processor's work bowl. Its shape also allows the machine to process small batches, sometimes a problem with the wider processor bowl. Processor bowls may have a problem with liquid seeping from the base. This can't happen with a blender. However, it cannot whip egg whites or cream, which the mixer can do, and the processor is better for chopping, shredding, and grating.

Blenders may have as many as 16 speeds, including an on-off pulse action designed to give more control over food consistency. Most cooks will use only a few settings and ignore the rest. Some models come with small jars that substitute for the standard container. These jars are a good size for small portions (including baby food), and they come with covers so they can be stored in the refrigerator.

Do you need a blender? If you make a lot of purées for soups, sauces, ice creams, and sorbets, and have space for the blender, you'll find it useful. However, if you have room for only one appliance of this type—in your budget or on your kitchen counter—the food processor, although more expensive, is more versatile and therefore a better buy.

Start a meal with an appetizer, accompany a soup with a snack—bread and cheese are among the basic ingredients for the recipes in this chapter.

Appetizers, Soups & Snacks

Help for the busy cook starts with appetizers (pages 18-20): Use the food processor or blender to make a dip, let the microwave soften cheese for Fruited Brie, or make flavored pecans ahead and refrigerate or freeze. Chicken Stock and Shortcut Beef Broth (page 24) are the basis of a wide variety of light soups (pages 20-27) and hearty main-dish soups (pages 28-33), most of which can be made in a microwave. Serve a light soup as a first course, or pair it with a salad, sandwich, or snack (see pages 34-35) for lunch or supper; the hearty soups are a meal in themselves.

Tiny Potato Appetizers are capped with sour cream and bits of chive and olive. Mix mustard or horseradish into the sour cream for a zesty accent.

APPETIZERS

Even the busy cook can entertain with style, using the recipes that follow. Some can be prepared ahead; some take only minutes to make, with helpers such as the microwave oven and the food processor. All allow you to offer a tasty nibble to your guests without spending hours in the kitchen.

HUMMUS

Serve this Middle Eastern dip with fresh raw vegetable pieces, cracker bread, or toasted pita bread. Sesame tahini, which is ground from sesame seeds and has the consistency of peanut butter, is available in many supermarkets and specialty food stores. If it has separated, stir it well before using. Peanut butter can be substituted for the tahini, if necessary.

> 2 cans (15 oz each) garbanzo beans
> 3 cloves garlic
> 2 tablespoons lemon juice, or more to taste
> 6 tablespoons sesame tahini or 2 to 3 tablespoons peanut butter
> ¼ teaspoon ground cumin, or to taste (optional)
> Salt to taste
> Finely chopped parsley, for garnish

1. Drain liquid from 1 can garbanzo beans and put beans in a food processor or blender. Add remaining can garbanzo beans with its liquid, garlic, lemon juice, and tahini, and process until smooth.

2. Add cumin (if used) and salt to taste and process or blend a few seconds more. Serve in a bowl garnished with parsley.

Makes 3 cups.

Preparation Time About 10 minutes

Timesaver Tip Recipe can be made 3 to 4 days ahead and stored, covered, in refrigerator. Serve at room temperature.

PUERTO VALLARTA DIP

The fresh cilantro *makes* this dip! Chile salsa is available in varying degrees of fieriness; add it to taste.

> 1 can (6½ oz) tuna, *drained*
> 1 green onion, *sliced*
> 1 to 3 tablespoons hot chile salsa
> 3 to 4 tablespoons mayonnaise
> 6 to 8 cilantro sprigs, or to taste, chopped
> Lemon or lime juice to taste
> Salt to taste
> Tortilla chips

In a bowl stir together tuna, onion, salsa, mayonnaise (water-pack tuna may require more mayonnaise), and cilantro. Season to taste with lemon juice and salt; adjust other-seasonings to taste. Serve with chips.

Makes about 1½ cups.

Preparation Time About 10 minutes

Timesaver Tip Recipe can be prepared in processor. Cut green onion into 1-inch lengths and put in processor fitted with steel blade. Add

cilantro sprigs and process for 3 to 5 seconds. Add tuna, salsa, mayonnaise, lemon juice, and salt; pulse a few times to combine. Taste, adjust seasoning, and pulse one or two times more. Recipe can be made 4 or 5 hours ahead and stored, covered, in refrigerator. Remove from refrigerator about 30 minutes before serving.

TINY POTATO APPETIZERS

Save vitamin-enriched water from boiling potatoes for soups, or seal in vitamins by baking in the microwave.

> 12 new red-skinned potatoes, approximately 1½ inches in diameter
> Freshly ground black pepper
> ½ cup sour cream
> 2 to 3 tablespoons chopped ripe black olives
> 2 to 3 tablespoons finely chopped chives or *1 large green onion top, finely chopped*
> Watercress or parsley, for garnish

1. Cook potatoes in boiling water until tender. *Or,* prick skins with a fork to release steam, and microwave on 100% power about 12 minutes.

2. Slice potatoes in half crosswise. Remove a small scoop from each half with a melon baller or small spoon.

3. Grind pepper onto potatoes. Fill each hollow with a dollop of sour cream and top with ripe olives and chives. Serve on a bed of watercress.

Makes 2 dozen.

Preparation Time 20 to 30 minutes

Variation For a change of pace, mix sour cream with Dijon mustard or horseradish to taste.

FRUITED BRIE

This cheese-with-a-difference is a snap to make in the microwave. Offer the Brie at a cocktail party with crackers or sliced baguettes.

> 2 tablespoons brandy
> 3 tablespoons golden raisins
> 1 tablespoon currants or dark raisins
> 1 wheel (8 oz) Brie
> 2 tablespoons chopped toasted walnuts

1. Place brandy, raisins, and currants in a small bowl. Microwave on 100% power until raisins absorb brandy, 30 to 60 seconds.

2. Place Brie in a microwave-safe serving dish. Microwave on 100% power until cheese is warmed and begins to melt (30 to 60 seconds). Sprinkle raisins and walnuts on top of Brie.

Serves 6 to 8.

Preparation Time 5 to 10 minutes

DIJON CRÈME

Lemon and Dijon mustard add a light and refreshing touch to this crème. It serves to enhance—not mask—flavors; offer it spread over smoked salmon, spears of baby asparagus, or as a vegetable dip with a cool glass of Chardonnay.

> ½ cup mayonnaise
> 1½ to 2 tablespoons Dijon mustard
> 1 tablespoon lemon juice, or to taste
> ⅓ cup whipping cream

1. In a bowl blend together mayonnaise, mustard, and lemon juice.

2. In a deep bowl whip cream until soft peaks form. Fold into mayonnaise mixture.

Makes about ¾ cup.

Preparation Time About 10 minutes

MUSTARD-DILL SAUCE

Serve this tangy sauce atop smoked salmon as an appetizer course. It also makes a good dip for fresh vegetables and cooked shrimp.

2 tablespoons Dijon mustard
1 tablespoon white wine vinegar
1 to 1½ tablespoons sugar
3 to 4 tablespoons chopped fresh dill or 1½ teaspoons dried
½ cup light olive oil or vegetable oil

In a bowl whisk together mustard, vinegar, sugar, and dill. Slowly whisk in oil until mixture is blended and thickens slightly. Adjust flavors to taste.

Makes about ⅔ cup.

Preparation Time About 5 minutes

CHUTNEY PECANS

A generous coating of spices gives these pecans a memorable snap.

¼ cup butter or margarine
¼ cup vegetable oil
¼ cup brown sugar
3 tablespoons curry powder
1 tablespoon ground ginger
⅛ to ¼ teaspoon cayenne pepper
1½ pounds pecan halves
⅓ cup chutney, finely chopped
Salt to taste

1. Preheat oven to 350° F. In a large skillet over medium heat, heat butter and oil until butter melts.

2. Stir in brown sugar, curry powder, ginger, and cayenne. Add pecans and stir until well coated.

3. Add chutney to pan and mix well. Salt to taste.

4. Line two baking sheets with paper towels. Spread pecans in pan. Bake until pecans are toasted, 10 to 15 minutes.

5. Remove pecans from paper towels and let cool. (Do not let pecans cool on paper towels or they will stick.)

Makes about 7 cups.

Preparation Time About 30 minutes.

Timesaver Tip Nuts can be made up to a week ahead and stored, covered, in refrigerator. Nuts can also be frozen up to 2 months.

SKEWERED TORTELLINI APPETIZER

For a festive look, garnish the tortellini with red bell peppers or cherry tomatoes, or serve them on a brightly colored platter.

Mild Vinaigrette (see page 99)
1 package (10 or 12 oz) frozen tortellini
2 tablespoons finely chopped fresh basil or parsley

1. Prepare Mild Vinaigrette.

2. Cook tortellini following package directions. Drain.

3. Toss warm tortellini with Mild Vinaigrette. Place in a covered container and let stand at room temperature at least 30 minutes before serving.

4. With a slotted spoon, drain tortellini and thread on short bamboo skewers, two tortellini to each skewer. Arrange on a serving platter and sprinkle with chopped basil.

Serves 8 to 12.

Preparation Time About 30 minutes

Timesaver Tip Appetizer can be made up to 24 hours ahead and stored, covered, in refrigerator. About 1 hour before serving, remove tortellini from refrigerator and allow them to reach room temperature, then transfer to skewers.

APPETIZER AND LIGHT-MEAL SOUPS

An appetizer soup is a comforting beginning to a meal when the weather is cold, a refreshing start when it's hot. The same soup is often just right for lunch or a light supper, paired with a sandwich or one of the snacks on pages 34–35. Recipes for hearty, sustaining soups that are a meal in themselves can be found on pages 28–33.

The soups that follow are tasty, nourishing, and healthful—low in sodium, fat, and calories. All are made from scratch; most start from a beef or chicken stock base.

Homemade chicken stock does require several hours of simmering, but it is otherwise easy to make. Since it freezes beautifully, you can make a large batch when you have some time, and let the freezer supply you for weeks to come. When you're out of homemade stock and time is too short to make more, canned chicken broth is an acceptable substitute. Be aware though, that most canned broths are highly salted. Low-sodium chicken broth, which is widely available in supermarkets today, is a recommended alternative for homemade chicken stock.

Unfortunately, the canned beef broths on the market today are unsatisfactory. However, Shortcut Beef Broth (page 24) can be prepared in about one hour. The key to this recipe is to chop the ingredients finely; this exposes more surface area, so flavor is released quickly.

All the appetizer soups can be reheated in the microwave oven. Microwave them at 70% power until they are heated through.

WILD RICE AND MUSHROOM SOUP

This earthy soup uses both fresh and dried mushrooms. Serve it as the first course of a hearty winter meal.

- ½ cup (about ½ oz) dried mushrooms, such as porcini or morels
- 4 cups chicken or beef stock or 3 cans (10½ oz each) low-sodium chicken broth
- 1½ cups sliced fresh mushrooms
  Half a large onion, chopped
- ⅓ cup wild rice, rinsed
  Salt and freshly ground pepper to taste
  Sour cream
  Chopped parsley, for garnish (optional)

1. Cover dried mushrooms with hot tap water and soak for about 15 minutes while preparing other ingredients.

2. In a large saucepan combine stock, sliced fresh mushrooms, onion, and wild rice. Bring to a boil. Reduce heat and simmer, uncovered.

3. Meanwhile, remove dried mushrooms from soaking liquid, reserving liquid. Add mushrooms to soup. Strain soaking liquid through cheesecloth and add to saucepan. Continue cooking until wild rice is tender, 35 to 45 minutes total cooking time. Season to taste with salt and pepper.

4. Ladle soup into individual bowls. Add a spoonful of sour cream to each and sprinkle with parsley, if desired.

Serves 4 to 6.

Preparation Time 45 to 50 minutes

Timesaver Tip Recipe can be made up to 1 day in advance and reheated.

Microwave Version

1. Complete step 1 as directed above.

2. In a 2-quart casserole combine stock, sliced fresh mushrooms, onion, and wild rice. Cover. Microwave on 100% power until broth boils, 5 to 6 minutes.

3. Simmer on 30% power 35 to 45 minutes. Continue with steps 3 and 4. Preparation time and timesaver tip same as above.

Wild Rice and Mushroom Soup is a rich blend of dried mushrooms (porcini or morels), fresh mushrooms, wild rice, and stock. An added plus: The soup can be prepared a day in advance.

GINGER CRAB SOUP

Bright green snow peas and shreds of orange carrot color this delicate clear soup, a beautiful first course for an elegant dinner.

> 3 cups homemade chicken stock or 2 cans (10½ oz each) chicken broth, preferably low-sodium, plus water to make 3 cups
>
> 2 thin slices unpeeled fresh ginger
>
> 1 small carrot
>
> ¼ pound snow peas
>
> 4 to 6 ounces fresh crabmeat or frozen crabmeat, thawed
>
> 1 green onion, chopped, or 2 tablespoons coarsely chopped chives
>
> 2 tablespoons dry sherry, or to taste
>
> ½ to 1 teaspoon white vinegar, or to taste
>
> Salt and cayenne pepper to taste

1. In a medium saucepan, bring chicken stock and ginger to a simmer.

2. Peel carrot and cut into 1½- to 2-inch-long julienne strips, the size of thin noodles. Remove strings from snow peas; cut snow peas on the diagonal into 1-inch pieces.

3. Drop carrots into simmering broth; simmer 30 seconds.

4. Remove pan from heat and remove ginger slices.

5. Stir in snow peas, crabmeat, and onions. Season to taste with sherry, vinegar, salt, and cayenne.

Serves 3 to 4.

Preparation Time About 15 minutes

Microwave Version

1. Peel carrot and cut into 1½- to 2-inch-long julienne strips, the size of thin noodles. Remove strings from snow peas; cut snow peas on the diagonal into 1-inch pieces.

2. Place chicken stock and ginger in 2-quart casserole. Cover tightly and microwave on 100% power to boiling, 4 to 6 minutes.

3. Add carrots to broth. Microwave on 100% power 30 seconds.

4. Remove ginger slices. Continue with step 5 as directed above. Serve immediately. Preparation time same as above.

HOT AND SOUR SOUP

You get to choose how "hot" with this oriental favorite. Swirls of color from carrots and green onions, barely cooked, add a festive look.

> 4 cups homemade chicken stock or 3 cans (10½ oz each) chicken broth, preferably low-sodium
>
> 1½ tablespoons cornstarch
>
> 1¼ teaspoons freshly ground black pepper, or more to taste
>
> ¼ cup rice vinegar
>
> 1 to 2 teaspoons soy sauce
>
> 1 teaspoon sesame oil
>
> 1 large or 2 small carrots cut into 2-inch-long julienne strips (about 1 cup)
>
> 4 to 5 medium green onions cut diagonally (about ¾ cup)
>
> 6 ounces tiny (bay) shrimp or crabmeat

1. Heat chicken stock in a saucepan over medium heat.

2. Combine cornstarch and pepper in a small bowl. Whisk in vinegar, soy sauce, and sesame oil.

3. Pour cornstarch mixture into hot chicken stock, whisking to blend. Bring mixture to a boil; boil 1 minute. Remove from heat.

4. Stir carrots into broth and simmer for about 3 minutes.

5. Stir green onions and shrimp into soup. Remove from heat. Adjust flavors to taste.

Serves 4 to 6.

Preparation Time 20 to 25 minutes

Ginger Crab Soup is composed of crabmeat, snow peas, and julienned carrot in a chicken stock subtly flavored with ginger.

Homemade chicken and beef stock are the backbone of outstanding soups, and well worth the time it takes to simmer them to flavorful perfection. Here, Japanese Clear Soup, based on Chicken Stock.

CHICKEN STOCK

To make stock, freeze chicken parts—back, neck, and giblets (except liver)—in a heavy plastic bag up to three months. Stock can be frozen up to eight months.

> 5 *pounds chicken parts—backs, necks, wings, giblets (do not use livers), and bones*
> 16 *cups water*
> 2 *medium onions, peeled and quartered*
> 2 *carrots, chopped*
> 2 *celery stalks, chopped*
> 8 *peppercorns*
> 6 *sprigs parsley*
> 2 *bay leaves*
> *Several sprigs fresh thyme or ½ teaspoon dried*
> 2 *whole cloves*

1. Place chicken parts in a large pot, cover with the water and bring to a gentle boil; skim foam as it rises.

2. Reduce heat, add remaining ingredients, and simmer 3 to 4 hours. Skim foam occasionally.

3. Strain stock through a cheese-cloth-lined colander or wire-mesh sieve. Cool to room temperature. To use broth immediately, blot up liquid fat from surface by touching the globules lightly with a paper towel. If you're not using it the same day, refrigerate; spoon off the fat when it solidifies on the surface.

4. Store in refrigerator for several days, or freeze up to 8 months.

Makes 16 cups.

Preparation Time 3 to 4 hours, including simmering

SHORTCUT BEEF BROTH

This is lighter in body than the classic version, but it's much faster to prepare. Make a large quantity and freeze it for later use.

> 2 *pounds lean boneless beef, finely chopped or ground*
> 1 *large onion, finely chopped*
> 2 *carrots, finely chopped*
> 1 *celery stalk, finely chopped*
> 2 *whole cloves*
> 4 *whole peppercorns*
> 5 *or 6 parsley sprigs*
> 8 *cups water*

1. Combine all ingredients in a large pot. Bring to a simmer, stirring once or twice. Do not boil.

2. Partially cover pan and simmer gently for 45 minutes. Do not stir or skim broth while it cooks.

3. Strain broth through a cheese-cloth-lined colander or wire-mesh sieve. To use broth immediately, blot up liquid fat from surface by touching the globules lightly with a paper towel. If you're not using it the same day, refrigerate it; spoon off the fat when it solidifies on the surface.

4. Store in refrigerator several days, or freeze up to 8 months.

Makes 8 cups.

Preparation Time About 1 hour

SPICY PEAR SOUP

In the fall, you can serve this soup warm; in the summer it's refreshing chilled.

    2 ripe pears, about 1 pound
       (see Note)
    ¼ teaspoon ground cinnamon,
       or more to taste
    ¼ teaspoon ground ginger,
       or more to taste
       About 1½ cups cranberry juice
       Low-fat plain yogurt, for
       garnish

1. Peel and core the pears; coarsely chop them.

2. In a medium saucepan combine pears, cinnamon, ginger, and 1½ cups cranberry juice. Simmer until soft (cooking time will vary depending on type of pears used).

3. Drain pears, reserving liquid.

4. Purée pears in food processor or blender. With machine running, slowly add cooking liquid.

5. Return to saucepan. Add more cranberry juice if soup is too thick. Adjust spices to taste.

6. Soup may be served warm, or refrigerated and served cold. Garnish each serving with a dollop of yogurt.

Serves 4.

Preparation Time 20 to 30 minutes

Note Very ripe Bartlett pears are soft enough not to require cooking. Chop pears coarsely and put them in food processor or blender with cinnamon, ginger, and 1½ cups cranberry juice. Purée pears and continue with step 5.

Microwave Version

1. Peel and core the pears; coarsely chop them.

2. Combine pears, cinnamon, ginger, and 1½ cups cranberry juice in a 2-quart casserole. Cover. Microwave on 100% power 3 to 5 minutes, or until pears are soft (cooking time will vary depending on type of pear used). Continue with step 3 above. Preparation time same as above.

JAPANESE CLEAR SOUP

This easy soup, which is elegant for entertaining, can be prepared ahead and reheated.

    4 cups homemade chicken stock
       or 3 cans (10½ oz each)
       chicken broth, preferably
       low-sodium
    3 to 4 tablespoons dry sherry
    1 to 2 tablespoons soy sauce
       (use smaller amount if
       chicken broth is not
       low-sodium)
       Garnishes: tofu, cut into
       bite-sized cubes (4 or 5
       cubes per serving); 3 to 4
       mushrooms, thinly sliced; 1
       green onion, finely chopped;
       half a carrot, shredded;
       half a lemon, thinly sliced

1. In a large saucepan bring chicken stock to a simmer. Stir in sherry and soy sauce. Simmer several minutes.

2. Arrange your choice of garnishes in small bowls to pass at the table. Ladle broth into soup bowls and serve.

Serves 4.

Preparation Time 10 to 15 minutes

Microwave Version

1. Place chicken stock in a deep 2-quart casserole. Microwave, uncovered, on 100% power until stock boils, about 5 to 7 minutes.

2. Stir in sherry and soy sauce. Microwave on 30% power 2 minutes.

3. Continue with step 2. Preparation time same as above.

GINGER-CURRY PUMPKIN SOUP

Be bold with the cayenne pepper—it really zips up the soup.

    1 can (16 oz) pumpkin
    2½ cups homemade chicken stock
       or 2 cans (10½ oz each)
       chicken broth, preferably
       low-sodium
    1 teaspoon finely grated or
       minced ginger
    ¾ to 1 teaspoon curry powder,
       or to taste
       Salt and cayenne pepper
       to taste
       Toasted pumpkin seeds or
       toasted sliced almonds, for
       garnish (optional)

1. In a medium saucepan combine pumpkin, stock, ginger, and curry powder. Bring to a boil. Reduce heat and simmer 3 minutes. Season to taste with salt and cayenne.

2. Ladle soup into serving bowls and garnish with pumpkin seeds, if desired.

Serves 4 to 5.

Preparation Time 8 to 10 minutes

Timesaver Tip Recipe can be prepared several days ahead and reheated in a saucepan over low heat or in the microwave oven.

Microwave Version

1. Combine pumpkin, stock, ginger, curry powder, and cayenne in a deep 2-quart casserole. Microwave, uncovered, on 100% power until soup boils, about 3 to 5 minutes.

2. Microwave on 30% power 2 minutes.

3. Continue with step 2. Preparation time and timesaver tip same as above.

For Speedy Spinach Soup, fresh spinach is puréed with chicken stock, mixed with cream, and enlivened with a touch of dill.

SPEEDY SPINACH SOUP

The food processor eases preparation of this emerald-green soup—it allows you to eliminate cooking the spinach. If you leave out the cream, the soup is low in calories: about 55 per serving based on 5 servings; about 45 per serving based on 6 servings.

> 5 cups homemade chicken stock
> or 4 cans (10½ oz each)
> chicken broth, preferably
> low-sodium
> 1 large bunch fresh spinach,
> rinsed and stemmed,
> or 1 package (10 oz)
> frozen chopped spinach,
> thawed
> ⅓ cup whipping cream or
> half-and-half
> 1 to 1½ teaspoons finely
> chopped fresh dill or ¼ to
> ½ teaspoon dried
> Salt and freshly ground
> black pepper to taste

1. In a medium saucepan, bring stock to a boil.

2. Place spinach in food processor fitted with the steel blade, or in a blender. With motor running, add about 2 cups stock to spinach. Process about 60 seconds.

3. Return spinach mixture to saucepan. Stir in remaining stock and the cream. Cook until soup is heated through. Season to taste with dill, salt, and pepper.

Serves 5 to 6.

Preparation Time About 15 minutes

Microwave Tip Frozen spinach can be thawed in microwave oven on Defrost setting.

Microwave Version

1. Place stock in deep 2-quart casserole. Microwave on 100% power 3 to 5 minutes, until it boils. Continue with step 2.

2. Return spinach mixture to casserole. Stir in cream. Microwave on 100% power 1 to 2 minutes to heat through. Season to taste with dill, salt, and pepper. Preparation time same as above.

GREEN GARDEN SOUP

Potato thickens this soup and gives it a pleasing texture.

> 1 white or red potato,
> approximately ½ pound
> 1 green onion, chopped, or
> half a medium onion, chopped
> 1½ cups homemade chicken
> stock or 1 can (10½ oz)
> chicken broth, preferably
> low-sodium
> 1 bunch (approximately 12
> to 14 oz) fresh spinach,
> well washed, trimmed and
> coarsely chopped, or 1 pack-
> age (10 oz) frozen
> chopped spinach (see Note)
> ¾ teaspoon minced fresh dill
> or ⅛ to ¼ teaspoon dried, or
> to taste
> ½ cup half-and-half
> Salt and freshly ground
> pepper to taste

1. Peel potato and cut into chunks.

2. Put potato and onions in a medium saucepan with chicken broth. Cover and bring to a boil. Reduce heat and simmer 10 to 15 minutes, until potatoes are tender.

3. Remove from heat; stir in spinach and dill.

4. Transfer mixture to a food processor or blender and process until smooth.

5. Return mixture to saucepan. Stir in half-and-half. Add more half-and-half, stock, or water if soup is too thick. Season to taste with salt and pepper.

Serves 4 to 5.

Preparation Time 20 to 25 minutes

Microwave Version

1. Peel potato and cut into chunks. Put potatoes and onion in 2-quart microwave-safe casserole with 1½ cups chicken broth. Cover. Microwave on 100% power 3 to 5 minutes, until broth boils.

2. Microwave on 100% power 7 to 10 minutes, until potatoes are tender. Continue with step 3. Preparation time: 15 to 20 minutes

Note If you are using frozen spinach, partially thaw it and then cut it into chunks. Add chunks to pan several minutes before potatoes are done, and cook until spinach is totally thawed and heated through.

MAIN-MEAL SOUPS

Full-meal soups originated as thrifty peasant dishes that could be prepared with a minimum of fuel and utensils. A basic, comforting food, soup brought the family together in communion around the stewing pot. You'll find the following soups nourishing, hearty, and simple to make when you're short on time. Combined with a crusty roll and a salad, they make a light yet filling meal.

These soups are based on chicken or beef stock (see page 24 for recipes for Chicken Stock and Shortcut Beef Broth). Canned chicken broth, preferably that which is labeled low-sodium, is an acceptable substitute for homemade. However, canned beef broth is not recommended.

SICILIAN-STYLE CLAM SOUP

This is a quick, last-minute soup, made from ingredients kept on hand. A healthy pinch of cayenne, and a parsley-garlic mixture added at the table, enliven the soup's flavor and color.

    1 can (15 oz) stewed tomatoes
    2 cans (6 oz each) chopped
       clams
    1 cup water
    ¼ teaspoon dried oregano
    ¼ teaspoon dried basil
       Pinch cayenne pepper
    2 tablespoons finely chopped
       parsley
    ¼ to ½ teaspoon minced garlic

1. Pour tomatoes into a medium saucepan and break them up into small pieces.

2. Stir in clams and their juice, then add the water, oregano, basil, and cayenne.

3. Bring soup to a simmer over medium heat. Simmer gently about 5 minutes.

4. Combine parsley and garlic. To serve, ladle soup into wide shallow soup bowls. At the table sprinkle parsley-garlic mixture over each serving.

Serves 4.

Preparation Time About 15 minutes

Microwave Version

Complete steps 1 and 2 as directed above, using a 2-quart bowl. Microwave on 70% power 5 minutes. Continue with step 4.

CHICKEN SOUP WITH LEMON AND MINT

Without the enrichment of egg yolks and cream this is a light chicken soup sparked by the flavoring of mint and lemon. Add the enrichment for a silky texture and a more rounded flavor.

    5 cups homemade chicken stock
       or 4 cans (10½ oz each)
       chicken broth, preferably
       low-sodium
       Half a medium onion,
       chopped
    1 chicken breast (¾ lb), skinned
    ¼ cup long-grain rice
    3 to 4 teaspoons lemon juice
    2 to 4 teaspoons finely chopped
       fresh mint, or ¾ to 1½
       teaspoon dried
       Salt and freshly ground
       pepper to taste
       Lemon slices, for garnish

Enrichment *(optional)*

    2 egg yolks
    ¼ cup whipping cream

1. Combine stock and onion in large saucepan. Bring to a boil.

2. Add chicken breast and rice. Reduce heat. Cover and simmer 15 minutes. Remove chicken. If rice is not tender, continue cooking until it is tender.

3. When chicken is cool enough to handle, cut meat into large pieces. Return to broth.

4. Remove soup from heat. Stir in lemon juice, mint, and salt and pepper to taste.

5. *To serve without enrichment:* Ladle soup into serving bowls and float a lemon slice on each bowl.

6. *Or, to enrich soup:* Beat egg yolks and cream together in a small bowl. Slowly beat ¼ cup broth into egg mixture. Remove saucepan from heat, stir egg mixture into soup, and return pan to heat. Cook and stir until soup is hot; do not boil. Soup will not thicken, but the enrichment will give it more body. Adjust mint and lemon to taste. Ladle soup into serving bowls and float a lemon slice on each.

Serves 4.

Preparation Time About 45 minutes

Microwave Version

In step 1, combine stock and onion in a 2-quart bowl, cover with plastic wrap, and microwave on 100% power about 8 to 10 minutes. Add rice and chicken breast and microwave, covered, on 70% power 15 minutes. Remove chicken and, if necessary, continue to cook rice until done. Continue with step 3. Serve as directed in step 5, or enrich soup and serve as directed in step 6. Preparation time same as above.

TORTELLINI IN BROTH

In this light soup, tortellini swim in a low-calorie broth. Tortellini package sizes may vary in different parts of the country; use the nearest equivalent.

  5½ cups homemade chicken stock
        or 4 cans (10½ oz each)
        chicken broth, preferably
        low-sodium
    1 package (12 oz) frozen
        tortellini or 1 package (7 oz)
        dried tortellini, with meat or
        cheese filling
    1 medium zucchini, grated
    1 tomato, chopped
        Salt and freshly ground
        pepper to taste
        Freshly grated Parmesan
        cheese, for garnish

1. Bring chicken stock to a boil in a large saucepan.

2. Add tortellini. Simmer, timing according to package directions. Remove pan from heat.

3. Stir in zucchini and tomato. Season to taste with salt and pepper.

4. Ladle soup into wide shallow bowls. Pass Parmesan cheese at table.

Serves 4.

Preparation Time About 20 minutes

Microwave Version

Put stock in a microwave-safe 2-quart bowl and microwave on 100% power until it boils, about 8 to 10 minutes. Add tortellini and microwave on 70% power until tortellini are tender, timing according to package directions (the same as for on top of the stove). Continue with steps 3 and 4. Preparation time same as above.

A creamy version of that old favorite, chicken soup with rice, Chicken Soup With Lemon and Mint features a zesty flavor combination that makes it all new.

Sopa Seca, made with pasta cooked in broth until most of the liquid has been absorbed, can contain almost any vegetable, plus chicken or beef.

TEX-MEX BEAN SOUP

Chile salsa adds a kick to this hearty soup. Since different types of salsa vary in their degree of hotness, add this ingredient to taste. Serve the soup with warmed tortillas, tortilla chips, or Cheese Crisps, page 35, for a quick meal.

> 1 can (15 oz) stewed tomatoes
> 1 can (15 oz) kidney beans, drained
> 1½ cups homemade chicken stock or 1 can (10½ oz) chicken broth, preferably low-sodium
> 2 tablespoons chile salsa, or to taste
> Salt to taste
> Garnishes: shredded Cheddar or jack cheese, chopped green onions, sliced ripe olives, sour cream

1. Pour tomatoes into a large saucepan and break them up into small pieces.

2. Add beans, chicken stock, and chile salsa. Cook to heat through.

3. Season to taste with salt. Ladle into soup bowls and pass your choice of garnishes.

Serves 4.

Preparation Time About 10 minutes

Microwave Version

Complete steps 1 and 2 as directed above, using a microwave-safe 2-quart bowl. Microwave on 100% power 3 to 5 minutes and serve as directed in step 3. Preparation time same as above.

SOPA SECA

Mexican meals often include *sopas secas* ("dry soups"). Served without a broth, a sopa seca is usually made with rice or pasta. This is a great dish for using up leftover bits of vegetables, chicken, or beef. Serve it as a simple main dish with a green salad.

> 1 tablespoon vegetable oil
> ½ package (5 oz) coiled capellini or vermicelli
> Half an onion, finely chopped
> 1 clove garlic, minced
> Half a medium green bell pepper, seeded and diced
> 1 large tomato, diced
> 2 cups homemade beef or chicken stock or 1 can (10½ oz) chicken broth, plus enough water to make 2 cups
> Salt and freshly ground pepper to taste
> Freshly grated Parmesan or Romano cheese, for garnish

1. In a deep skillet over medium heat, heat oil. Break pasta into short lengths and carefully brown in hot oil (it burns easily).

2. Push pasta to one side and add onion, garlic, and bell pepper. Cook over medium heat until onion is translucent.

3. Add tomato and stock. Cover and cook until liquid is almost absorbed and pasta is tender (about 5 minutes). Taste; add salt and pepper as needed.

4. Serve with a sprinkling of cheese.

Serves 4.

Preparation Time 20 to 25 minutes

Variation For a delicious "wet" soup, increase the chicken or beef stock to 4 to 5 cups. Cook until pasta is tender.

HEARTY BLACK BEAN SOUP

This sturdy soup contains ham and tomatoes in addition to the beans, plus savory herbs and an enlivening touch of sherry. Add crusty rolls, a salad of fresh greens, and a beverage, and you have a meal.

    2 tablespoons oil
    3 medium onions, chopped
    4 cloves garlic, minced
    3 cans (16 oz each)
       black beans (frijoles
       negros), drained and rinsed
    1 tablespoon finely
       chopped fresh oregano or
       1 teaspoon dried, or to taste
    ½ teaspoon ground cumin, or
       to taste
    ½ teaspoon finely chopped
       fresh thyme or ¼ teaspoon
       dried, or to taste
    1 bay leaf
    2 cups cooked cubed ham
    2 cups chicken stock or 1
       can (10½ oz) chicken
       broth, preferably low-sodium,
       plus enough water to make
       2 cups
    ¼ cup dry sherry
    1 can (14½ or 16 oz)
       whole tomatoes, drained
       and chopped, or 1½ cups
       peeled, chopped fresh tomatoes
       Salt and freshly ground
       pepper to taste
       Accompaniments: fresh lime
       or lemon wedges, sour
       cream, thinly sliced
       radishes, sliced green onions,
       cilantro leaves, chile salsa

1. In a wide-bottomed, large sauce-pan over medium heat, heat oil. Add onions and cook until soft, 3 to 5 minutes. Add garlic and cook 1 min-ute longer.

2. Stir in beans, oregano, cumin, thyme, bay leaf, ham, stock, sherry, and tomatoes.

3. Increase heat and bring mixture to a boil. Reduce heat and simmer, uncovered, about 30 minutes. Season to taste with salt, if necessary, and pepper.

4. Serve soup with your choice of accompaniments, or cool to room temperature and refrigerate or freeze.

Makes about 7 cups (4 to 5 servings).

Preparation Time About 45 minutes

Timesaver Tip Soup can be made up to 2 days ahead, covered, and refrigerated, or it can be frozen. To freeze, spoon soup into one large or several smaller individual freez-er containers. Cover, label, and freeze at 0° F up to 1 month. To serve, defrost soup 15 to 20 minutes on Defrost setting of microwave, or thaw in refrigerator 8 to 24 hours. Gently warm soup in a saucepan or micro-wave at 50% power until it is warmed through. Stir several times both during defrosting and during reheating.

Microwave Version

Put oil in a 2-quart casserole and microwave on 70% power 45 sec-onds. Add onions and micro-wave another 3 minutes, until onions are soft. Add garlic and microwave a minute longer. Complete step 2 as directed above. Cover casserole with waxed paper or loosely with plastic wrap and microwave, still on 70% power, 30 minutes. Season to taste and proceed with step 4 as directed above. Preparation time and timesaver tip same as above.

SUNDAY NIGHT SEAFOOD STEW

This quick, one-pot dish allows you to take advantage of the freshest and best priced fish at the market—or you can use frozen fish. Serve it with good bread, a white wine, and a scrumptious dessert—perhaps Presto Pots de Crème (see page 112)—for an easy company dinner.

    1 bottle (8 oz) clam juice or
       1 can (12 oz) clam juice
    2 cups water
    ¾ to 1 teaspoon dried thyme
    ¼ teaspoon fennel seed, crushed
    1 bay leaf
    ½ to ¾ pound fresh or
       frozen skinless lean
       white fish—halibut,
       haddock, pollack,
       red snapper, whiting,
       bass, flounder, cod
       (see Note)
   12 to 16 medium shrimp,
       shelled and deveined,
       or mussels or clams,
       scrubbed, or 12 to 16
       of any combination
       of shellfish
    1 medium tomato, seeded
       and chopped
       Salt and freshly ground
       pepper to taste
       Finely chopped parsley, for
       garnish (optional)

1. In a large saucepan over high heat, combine clam juice, the water, thyme, fennel seeds, and bay leaf. Bring to a boil.

2. Reduce heat, cover, and simmer for 3 minutes.

3. Cut fish into 1-inch chunks. Add fish, shellfish, and tomatoes to broth. Gently simmer 3 to 5 minutes, until fish is opaque (mussels and clams will open and shrimp will turn pinkish and opaque).

4. Remove bay leaf; season to taste. Ladle soup into serving bowls. Garnish with parsley, if desired.

Serves 4.

Preparation Time About 20 minutes

Microwave Version

Combine ingredients as directed in step 1, using a 2-quart bowl. Microwave on 70% power 3 minutes. For step 3, after adding fish, shellfish, and tomatoes, microwave on 70% power 3 to 5 minutes. Serve as directed in step 4. Preparation time same as above.

<u>Note</u> If you are using frozen fish, partially defrost them, then cut into chunks—do not thaw completely. Add to broth before shellfish and simmer 3 to 5 minutes, then add shellfish and tomatoes and continue as directed in step 3.

A feast in a bowl, Sunday Night Seafood Stew can be made in the microwave oven. The recipe is flexible: You can use any combination of shellfish and firm white fish.

HOT GARLIC TOAST

A tasty accompaniment to soup, or the basis of a snappy appetizer, this toast will be best if made with good-quality bread and olive oil.

- 8 slices French or Italian bread
- 2 cloves garlic, peeled and sliced lengthwise
- 3 to 4 tablespoons olive oil

1. Preheat oven to 400°F. Rub both sides of bread slices with cut garlic. Brush with olive oil.

2. Place bread on a baking sheet. Bake 10 to 15 minutes until bread is toasted, turning once.

Serves 4.

Preparation Time About 20 minutes, including baking

Timesaver Tip Toast can be prepared 3 to 4 hours ahead through step 1.

TOASTY PITA TRIANGLES

Savory herbs and mellow Parmesan meld to make bite-size wedges. Serve as an accompaniment to soup or on their own as snacks.

- 3 tablespoons butter, softened
- 2 tablespoons chopped parsley or chives
- ½ teaspoon finely chopped fresh oregano or rosemary or ¼ teaspoon dried, or to taste
- 3 pita breads (7-inch diameter)
- 3 tablespoons freshly grated Parmesan cheese

1. Preheat oven to 450° F. Blend butter, parsley, and herbs.

2. Spread butter mixture on pita breads. Sprinkle tops with cheese.

3. Cut each pita into 6 triangles. Place on baking sheets. Bake until toasted, 10 to 15 minutes.

Serves 4 to 6.

Preparation Time About 20 minutes

Pita Pizzas offer an opportunity to use up leftover bits of meat and vegetables, or to try out new topping ideas. Here, anchovies, olives, chopped tomatoes, cheese, and herbs combine to make a savory snack.

SNACKS

These recipes don't call for hard-to-find ingredients or complicated procedures. In fact, many of the ingredients are likely to be staples in your pantry. Tasty but light, these are perfect for almost any time you want a snack, whether it's something to take along to the game or an after-school munchie. Paired with a soup or salad, they can complete the menu for a quick light dinner—after a hearty Sunday brunch, for instance. They're all quick to prepare and to clean up.

PITA PIZZAS

When baked at a high temperature, the pita-bread crust becomes crisp, just like a pizza at your local pizza parlor. The toppings, of course, can be as varied as your imagination. Consider, for instance, chopped fresh vegetables, bits of ham, or wedges of marinated artichoke hearts. Make a single pizza for a special lunch, or multiply the recipe to serve a whole crowd—try a party where the guests make their own pizzas with a colorful array of condiments.

For each pizza:

- 1 *pita bread (7- to 8-inch diameter)*
- 1 *teaspoon olive oil*
- ¼ *cup chopped, seeded tomatoes or 1 to 2 tablespoons tomato paste*
- ¼ *teaspoon finely chopped garlic Fresh or dried herbs (oregano, thyme, basil, and rosemary, singly or in combination)*
- 3 *to 4 tablespoons freshly grated Parmesan cheese Optional additional toppings: salami or pepperoni slices, onion rings, sliced olives, anchovies, other cheese such as mozzarella or goat cheese*

1. Preheat oven to the highest setting (450° F–550° F). Place the pita bread on a baking sheet and brush lightly with oil.

2. Top with tomatoes or spread with tomato paste.

3. Scatter garlic and your choice of fresh or dried herbs over top. Sprinkle with cheese.

4. Bake until crust is crisp and browned, 10 to 15 minutes.

Preparation Time About 25 minutes

BAGUETTE MELTS

Here's a no-fuss cheese snack you can serve hot from the oven.

- ½ *pound Cheddar cheese, shredded*
- 1 *can (4½ oz) chopped ripe olives*
- 1 *can (2 oz) diced pimientos*
- 4 *green onions, finely chopped*
- ½ *cup mayonnaise*
- 1½ *tablespoons prepared horseradish*
- 1 *large or 2 small baguettes, sliced diagonally*

1. Mix together cheese, olives, pimientos, green onions, mayonnaise, and horseradish.

2. Spoon about 1 tablespoon cheese mixture onto each baguette slice.

3. Broil until cheese starts to melt.

Makes 3 to 4 dozen.

Preparation Time About 30 minutes

Timesaver Tip Cheese topping can be made up to 2 days ahead, refrigerated, and used as needed.

GARLIC HERB BREAD

Perfect accompaniment for a watercress salad.

- 1 *small loaf (8 oz) French bread*
- ¼ *cup butter, softened*
- 1 *medium clove garlic, minced*
- 1 *to 1½ teaspoons finely chopped fresh oregano or ½ teaspoon dried*
- 2 *to 3 tablespoons grated Parmesan cheese*

1. Cut bread into 1½-inch-thick slices, or split lengthwise.

2. Blend together butter, garlic, and oregano. Spread on bread. Sprinkle with cheese.

3. Broil until top is light brown and bubbly, 2 to 3 minutes.

Makes about 12 slices, or two half-loaves (4 to 6 servings).

Preparation Time About 10 minutes

Microwave Version

1. Complete as directed in steps 1 and 2 above.

2. Place cut sides of bread back together to form loaf. Wrap in paper towel.

3. Microwave on 50% power until heated through, 30 to 60 seconds. Be careful not to overheat bread or it will get tough.

Preparation Time About 8 minutes

CHEESE CRISPS

For a terrific snack or light supper, try this variation on the open-faced toasted-cheese sandwich. Proportions of ingredients aren't important; experiment to find the combination that suits your taste. Note that if you're making lots of these, you can use your food processor to shred the cheese, mince the garlic, and slice the pitted olives.

For each crisp:

- 1 *flour tortilla Grated sharp Cheddar or jack cheese Minced garlic or garlic salt to taste Sliced black olives Chile salsa to taste Sour cream (optional)*

1. Preheat oven to 450° F. Place tortillas on baking sheets. Spread cheese on top. Sprinkle with garlic or garlic salt and scatter olives over top. Spoon on a few dollops of salsa.

2. Bake until tortillas are crisp and brown (about 10 minutes). Serve with sour cream, if desired.

Preparation Time 20 to 25 minutes

SOUP AND SANDWICH SUPPER

JB's Red Pepper Soup

Toasted Crab Rolls

Easy and Elegant Lemon
Mousse (page 114)

Beer

*Dinner isn't always
a formal, large
meal. Sometimes—
after a big noontime
Sunday dinner, for
example, or a
hearty brunch—all
that's needed is some
soup and a
sandwich. For such
an occasion, make
this distinctive
red pepper soup,
topped with sour
cream, and an open-
faced sandwich of
toasted crab and
cheese on
crusty rolls. For
dessert, enjoy an
airy lemon mousse.*

JB'S RED PEPPER SOUP

Many cooked-pepper dishes call for roasting and peeling the peppers. This time-consuming step is not required for the recipe below, which means the soup will have a nice nubby texture; if you prefer it smoother, strain it through a sieve.

  3 tablespoons butter or
     margarine
  4 medium red bell peppers,
     seeded and cut into strips
1½ cups chicken stock or
     1 can (10½ oz) chicken broth,
     preferably low-sodium, plus
     water to make 1½ cups
     Salt
  ⅛ teaspoon cayenne pepper,
     or to taste
     Sour cream

1. In a 3-quart saucepan over medium heat, melt butter. Add peppers.

2. Cover; cook peppers over medium heat until tender, about 8 minutes.

3. Pour peppers and liquid into a food processor or blender (if you use a blender, you may have to process in 2 batches). Process 2 minutes.

4. Return soup to pan and add chicken stock. Season to taste with salt and cayenne pepper; heat until hot.

5. Serve soup with a dollop of sour cream on top, or thin sour cream with milk or water and swirl it into soup. Do not stir.

Makes 4 cups, 4 to 6 servings.

Preparation Time About 20 minutes

Timesaver Tip Soup can be prepared through step 4 up to 3 days ahead and stored, covered, in refrigerator. To serve, heat and complete step 5.

Microwave Version

1. In a 2-quart casserole, microwave butter on 100% power 30 to 45 seconds, to melt. Add pepper strips.

2. Cover and microwave on 100% power until tender, about 5 minutes. Continue with step 3.

Preparation time 15 to 20 minutes

TOASTED CRAB ROLLS

These crab rolls are also good with Ginger-Curry Pumpkin Soup, page 25. For a pungent variation, substitute dill weed for the ground nutmeg.

  2 or 3 (6- to 7-inch)
     French rolls
     Melted butter or margarine
  ¾ pound fresh crabmeat or
     frozen crabmeat, thawed
  1 cup shredded Gruyère cheese
  1 large or 2 slender green
     onions, sliced
  ¼ cup mayonnaise
  2 tablespoons sour cream
     Cayenne pepper to taste
     Lemon juice to taste
     Ground nutmeg to taste

1. Preheat broiler. Split rolls in half lengthwise. Brush with melted butter. Lightly toast rolls under broiler. Preheat oven to 400° F.

2. Flake crabmeat, removing any cartilage. In a bowl, gently blend crabmeat, cheese, onions, mayonnaise, and sour cream. Season to taste with cayenne, lemon juice, and nutmeg.

3. Spoon crab mixture onto split toasted rolls and place rolls on baking sheets. Bake 5 to 10 minutes, or until sandwiches are hot.

Makes 6 rolls, 3 or 4 servings.

Preparation Time 20 to 25 minutes

Timesaver Tip Crab mixture can be made up to 6 hours ahead; reserve sliced green onions and mix in just before rolls are baked. Store prepared mixture, covered, in refrigerator.

A light supper combines home-made soup with miniature open-faced sandwiches. A mug of beer completes the menu.

*Baking starts with the basics—
flour, eggs, butter, brown
sugar—even for the timesaver
recipes in this chapter.*

Shortcut Baking

Home-baked goodies *are* possible for the busy cook, with the help of the microwave, freezer, and food processor. In this chapter, you'll find recipes for microwave baking (pages 41-43); for your own mixes to prepare in quantity and store for baking later (pages 49-52); and for make-'em-in-a-minute cookie favorites (pages 52-54). In addition, there are instructions for freezing batter, plus recipes (pages 43-49), and for shortcut yeast bread techniques, including mixing and kneading with the food processor, rising in the microwave oven, and freezing yeast doughs, followed by recipes (pages 54-61).

MICROWAVE MAKES IT EASY

Baking in a microwave oven produces mixed results. Many cakes, bar cookies, and brownies cook with speed and ease, and their taste, texture, and appearance are comparable—if not superior—to conventionally baked products. However, most cookies, pies, quick breads, and yeast breads are better when baked conventionally.

Microwaved cakes don't brown. In most cases, however, this is not really a disadvantage, since the cake can be topped with a frosting, a glaze, or a dusting of confectioners' sugar. Microwave baking has the advantage of producing cakes that are moist, airy, and light and have greater volume than those baked in a conventional oven. This is because the air inside a microwave oven is at room temperature and not hot and dry like the air in a conventional oven. Hot, dry air bakes a crust around the edges of the cake, restricting its volume.

The best cakes for microwaving are rich cakes made with whole eggs, pudding cakes, and cakes made with oil, such as the Carrot Cake on the facing page. Boxed cake mixes also can be microwaved with good results—just omit one egg when making the mix to improve texture and volume.

Round and ring shapes bake most evenly. Cakes often bake more evenly on the bottom when they're elevated on a plastic trivet or inverted glass dish. Rotating the cake dish once or twice, a quarter to a half turn, also facilitates an even doneness, especially in older ovens. When a cake is done, a toothpick or skewer inserted in the center will come out clean, and the edges will pull away from the sides of the pan.

Line round cake dishes with waxed paper to ease removal. Lightly grease fluted tube pans, or use a spray vegetable coating. Do not prepare pans with generous grease and flour—this creates a gummy surface.

Brownies and bar cookies exemplify the best of microwave baking. They look and taste good, and they cook in 6 to 10 minutes. Traditionally brownies and bar cookies are baked in square pans. To prevent the corners from overcooking in the microwave, shield the corners with triangles of foil. Remove the foil triangles about 2 minutes before the end of the baking time.

Fruit-based desserts, like the Apple-Ginger Crumble on page 43, have an excellent fresh flavor due to their fast cooking. Dessert sauces, which are often served with baked goods, cook evenly with a minimum of stirring because microwave energy heats all surfaces, not just the bottom of the dish.

Breads and rolls, even tortillas, can be defrosted and reheated in seconds in a microwave—in a basket or on a wooden board, if you wish. The secret is to reheat bread only until it's *warm*. Overheating will cook the bread, and it will come out of the microwave oven hard and tough. Also be aware that anything sugary—such as raisins, frostings, and jelly fillings—becomes hot very quickly. Use the chart above as a guide to reheating and defrosting breads, always checking at the minimum time.

What doesn't bake satisfactorily in a microwave? Yeast breads baked in a microwave oven are pale, low in volume, and tough. However, a microwave oven can save time during preparation. You can use your oven to melt butter, scald milk, or warm ingredients. And you can cut rising time by half or more when you follow the micro-rise method explained on page 57.

Most quick breads such as coffee cakes, biscuits, muffins, and nut breads are better baked conventionally. In the microwave oven they cook unevenly and end up pale, without the browned coloring we associate with properly cooked, good-tasting baked goods. Drop cookies cook so unevenly that they are not recommended for microwaving. Some burn while others are still doughy. Pie crusts don't brown or become crisp, although advocates of microwaved pie crusts feel that they are flakier than those cooked conventionally. Flans and dessert soufflés overcook on the edges before the center sets. Sheet cakes bake unevenly. Angel, sponge, and chiffon cakes, popovers, cream puffs, and meringues are unsuccessful because they require hot, dry air to set their structure.

REHEATING AND DEFROSTING BAKED GOODS AT 50% POWER

Servings	Starting at Room Temperature	Starting Frozen
1	10 to 30 seconds	30 seconds to 1 minute
2	15 to 40 seconds	45 seconds to 1¼ minutes
3	20 to 50 seconds	60 seconds to 1½ minutes
4	30 to 60 seconds	1½ to 2 minutes

CARROT CAKE WITH CREAM CHEESE HARD SAUCE

This recipe is ideal for microwave baking: It doesn't need surface browning, it's made with oil, and it bakes in a round container. You can grate the carrots in a food processor.

- 1½ cups flour
- 2¼ teaspoons ground cinnamon
- 1½ teaspoons baking soda
- ¾ teaspoon ground nutmeg
- ½ teaspoon salt
- 1½ cups sugar
- 1 cup vegetable oil
- 2 eggs
- 3 cups grated carrots (3 to 4 medium)
- 1 cup coarsely chopped walnuts

Cream Cheese Hard Sauce

- 1 package (3 oz) cream cheese, softened
- ¼ cup butter or margarine, softened
- 1 teaspoon vanilla extract
- 1½ cups confectioners' sugar, sifted

1. Combine flour, cinnamon, baking soda, nutmeg, and salt; set aside.

2. In a large bowl beat together sugar, oil, and eggs. Stir in carrots and nuts. Add dry ingredients; mix to combine thoroughly.

3. Lightly butter a ceramic or plastic fluted tube pan. Spoon in batter. Elevate pan on an inverted dish or plastic trivet.

4. Microwave on 50% power 18 to 24 minutes, rotating pan a half turn, if necessary, for even cooking. Cake will pull away slightly from the side of the pan when done, and a skewer inserted in the center will come out clean.

5. Cool slightly before inverting onto a serving plate. Serve with Cream Cheese Hard Sauce.

Serves 12.

Preparation Time About 35 minutes, including baking

Cream Cheese Hard Sauce With an electric mixer or by hand, cream together cream cheese, butter, and vanilla. Gradually beat in confectioners' sugar until smooth.
To make in food processor: Process cream cheese, butter, and vanilla. Add sugar all at once and process a few seconds. Cover and refrigerate to cool. Serve cool but not thoroughly chilled or sauce will be too hard to spoon and spread.

Makes about 2 cups.

Preparation Time 5 to 10 minutes

Microwave baking allows you to prepare nut-filled Carrot Cake in only 35 minutes. Serve it with Cream Cheese Hard Sauce, a snap to make with the help of an electric mixer or food processor.

MICROWAVE HELPS FOR BAKERS

Today's busy cooks may despair of finding the time to bake. But, as this chapter proves, baking doesn't have to be enormously time-consuming. Making good use of modern appliances can speed up the process. A microwave oven can help in a number of ways. Special low-heating microwave levels aren't necessary for the shortcuts listed below.

Toasting Coconut Spread 1 cup coconut in a thin layer in a glass pie plate. Microwave on 100% power until toasted (2 to 3 minutes). Stir every 30 seconds and watch carefully.

Melting Chocolate Squares Place 1 or 2 squares in a glass dish. Microwave on 50% power 2 to 5 minutes, stirring after 2 minutes.

Melting Chocolate Chips Place ½ to 1 cup chips in a glass dish. Microwave on 50% power 3 to 5 minutes. Stir until smooth.

Melting Butter or Margarine Place butter in a custard cup, glass measure, or casserole. Microwave on 100% power until butter melts (½ cup requires 45 to 60 seconds).

Softening Butter or Margarine For easy creaming or spreading, microwave butter on 50% power until softened (½ cup requires 10 to 20 seconds).

Softening Brown Sugar Place brown sugar in a glass bowl, or leave in plastic or cardboard package. Microwave on 100% power, checking every 30 seconds until softened.

Softening Cream Cheese Unwrap cream cheese and place in a glass dish or on a sheet of waxed paper. Microwave on 50% power until softened (3 ounces requires 30 to 45 seconds, 8 ounces, 60 to 90 seconds).

Warming Egg Whites If recipe calls for egg whites at room temperature, you can warm refrigerated eggs in the microwave. Place in microwave-safe bowl and heat on 100% power 15 seconds for 2 whites, 20 to 30 seconds for 4 whites.

Juicier Lemons Lemons yield more juice when slightly warm or at room temperature. If they've been in the refrigerator, microwave on 50% power 1 minute or longer to warm.

CHOCOLATE-COCONUT SQUARES

Very rich, and a hit with kids! This recipe works best in the microwave—it's quicker and easier than with a conventional oven, and the results are excellent.

> ½ cup butter or margarine, at room temperature
> 1 cup dark brown sugar
> 1 cup plus 2 tablespoons flour
> 2 eggs
> 1 teaspoon vanilla extract
> 1 cup chopped pecans or walnuts
> 1 cup flaked or shredded coconut
> 1 package (6 oz) semisweet chocolate chips (see Note)

1. Cream butter and ½ cup of the brown sugar until smooth. Add 1 cup of the flour and combine until mixture forms coarse crumbs. Press dough into an 8- or 9-inch square glass baking dish.

2. Microwave on 100% power 3 to 5 minutes, rotating dish if necessary for even doneness. Crust should lose all moist spots and look like a cooked pie shell (it will not brown).

3. Combine eggs, vanilla, nuts, coconut, chocolate chips, remaining flour, and remaining brown sugar.

4. Spread mixture over crust. Microwave on 100% power 4 to 5 minutes, until set, rotating dish if necessary for even doneness.

5. Cool on wire rack, then cut into squares.

Makes 16 squares.

Preparation Time 15 minutes, including baking

Note You can substitute butterscotch chips for the chocolate, or use a combination of both.

APPLE-GINGER CRUMBLE

Excellent with whipped cream, Crème Fraîche (see page 118), whipping cream, or cinnamon ice cream.

> 3 medium Granny Smith, pippin, or other tart apples, cored and sliced (about 1¼ pounds)
>
> 1½ to 2 tablespoons lemon juice
>
> ⅔ cup crushed gingersnap cookies (about 12 cookies)
>
> ⅔ cup rolled oats
>
> ¼ cup brown sugar
>
> ¼ cup butter or margarine, softened
>
> 1 teaspoon ground cinnamon

1. Sprinkle sliced apples with lemon juice. Place in a round or oval 9- or 10-inch glass baking dish.

2. Cut remaining ingredients together with a pastry blender or fork until crumbly. Sprinkle over fruit.

3. Microwave at 100% power until fruit is tender (7 to 9 minutes); give dish a half turn once. Serve warm.

Serves 5 to 6.

Preparation Time About 20 minutes, including baking

Variation Three to four pears may be substituted for apples.

BROWNIE BINGE

This is a very fudgy brownie. When cooked in a microwave oven, it is moister than most brownies.

> 1 cup butter or margarine
>
> 2 ounces unsweetened chocolate
>
> 1 cup sugar
>
> ½ cup flour
>
> 1 teaspoon baking powder
>
> 2 eggs
>
> 1 teaspoon vanilla extract
>
> ½ cup coarsely chopped walnuts or pecans
>
> 1 package (6 oz) semisweet chocolate chips

1. Place butter and chocolate in an 8- or 9-inch square glass baking dish. Microwave on 50% power 5 minutes, or until melted. Stir to combine.

2. Stir sugar, flour, and baking powder into butter mixture with a fork. Beat in eggs and vanilla until mixture forms a batter.

3. Sprinkle top with nuts and chocolate chips. Shield corners of dish with foil (see page 40).

4. Microwave on 50% power 12 to 15 minutes, turning if necessary to insure even doneness. Brownies are done when toothpick inserted in center comes out barely moist. Remove foil shields last 5 minutes of baking time.

5. Cool completely, then cut into squares.

Makes 16.

FROZEN BATTER TECHNIQUE

Freezing baked goods is nothing new, but freezing batters is! When you freeze batters ahead and bake them just before serving, you can save time and still enjoy that wonderful warm-from-the-oven flavor and aroma.

You simply prepare the batter—muffins, brownies, cakes, or quick breads—and freeze for up to four weeks, then bake as usual, increasing the baking time as the recipe directs. There's no thawing required; the batter goes directly from the freezer to the oven. The quality of baked goods is far superior when you freeze batters rather than the finished products. (You can, however, freeze finished baked goods too; see page 40 for instructions on using the microwave oven to defrost them.)

Try adapting your favorite quick bread recipes to this technique. The only adjustment you must make is in baking time—depending on the batter's density and the size of the baking dish, you will need to increase the baking time by 5 to 30 minutes.

The batter should be frozen in the pan in which it will be baked. To keep your pans free for other uses, first line them with heavy-duty foil, then pour in the batter and freeze it, uncovered, until it is solid. This usually takes 6 to 12 hours. Remove the batter from the pan and wrap it completely, label and date the package, and return it to the freezer. To bake, grease the baking pan in which the batter was frozen, peel away the foil, and place the batter back in the pan.

Proper packaging is important for protecting batters during storage. Package materials must be resistant to both moisture and air. Aluminum foil is excellent; use either heavy-duty foil or a double thickness of regular foil. Heavy plastic bags designed for freezer storage are suitable for packaging cupcakes, muffins, and quick breads. Be sure to check the label on the package—if it does not say the bags are suitable for freezing, choose another bag.

Air pockets between food and the package material collect moisture, resulting in frost and freezer burn. When wrapping frozen batters, press out as much air as you can and mold the wrapping as close to the food as possible. To extract air from plastic bags, insert a drinking straw in the opening, squeeze the opening shut around the straw, inhale to draw out the air, and fasten tightly. Be sure to label and date all packages.

Most batters will keep up to four weeks at 0° F. If your freezer doesn't maintain a temperature of 0° F (and many combination refrigerator-freezers don't), keep the batter frozen no more than two weeks.

SOUR CREAM FUDGE CAKE

If you find yourself cooking with chocolate often, consider buying it in bulk—it freezes well.

> 3 ounces unsweetened chocolate
> ½ cup hot water
> ¾ cup butter or margarine at room temperature
> 1¾ cups sugar
> 3 eggs
> 1 cup sour cream
> 2 cups cake flour
> 1¾ teaspoons baking powder
> 1 teaspoon baking soda
> ¼ teaspoon salt

Fudge Frosting

> 4 ounces unsweetened chocolate
> ½ cup butter or margarine
> 1 pound confectioners' sugar (3½ cups), sifted
> ¼ cup milk
> 2 teaspoons vanilla extract

1. Preheat oven to 375° F. Heat chocolate and water in top of a double boiler, stirring until mixture is smooth. Cool.

2. In large bowl of electric mixer, cream butter and sugar until light and fluffy. Add eggs, one at a time, beating after each addition. Stir sour cream into cooled chocolate mixture. Add to batter; mix just enough to blend.

3. Sift together flour, baking powder, baking soda, and salt. Add to batter; mix just until smooth.

4. *To make layer cake:* Grease two 8-inch round layer cake pans. Spoon batter into pans. Bake until a toothpick inserted in the center comes out clean, 45 to 50 minutes. Cool cake in pan 15 minutes; remove cake from pan and cool completely. *To make cupcakes:* Line muffin cups with cupcake liners; fill three-fourths full. Bake until toothpick inserted in center comes out clean, about 25 minutes. Cool completely.

5. Frost with Fudge Frosting.

Makes 1 two-layer cake or about 2 dozen cupcakes.

Fudge Frosting

1. Heat chocolate and butter in top of a double boiler, stirring until smooth. Cool.

2. In a medium bowl, beat sugar, milk, and vanilla until smooth. Stir in chocolate mixture.

3. Set bowl in pan of ice water and beat with a spoon or hand-held electric mixer until frosting is smooth and thick enough to spread. *Or refrigerate frosting until thick enough to spread; do not overchill.*

Timesaver Tip *Layer cakes:* Line two 8-inch round layer cake pans with heavy-duty aluminum foil. Spoon batter into pans and freeze until solid. Remove from pan and wrap. Label and date package, and freeze at 0° F up to 6 weeks. To bake, peel foil from batter and return, unthawed, to greased pans. Bake in a preheated 375° F oven until a toothpick inserted in the center comes out clean, 45 to 50 minutes. *Cupcakes:* Line muffin cups with cupcake liners and fill three-fourths full. Freeze until solid. Remove from pans and pack in freezer bags or heavy-duty aluminum foil. Label and date package and freeze at 0° F up to 6 weeks. To bake, place cupcakes in pan and bake in a preheated 375° F oven, unthawed, until a pick inserted in center comes out clean, about 25 minutes.

BABY CAKES

These individual cakes are baked in tin cans, then cut into layers and frosted. For a fun presentation, use pinking shears to cut out squares of colorful wrapping paper large enough to cover the center of your dessert plates. Serve the Baby Cakes on the wrapping-paper squares.

> ⅔ cup butter or margarine, softened
> 1¾ cups sugar
> 2 eggs
> 2 teaspoons vanilla extract
> 3 cups cake flour
> 2 teaspoons baking powder
> ¾ teaspoon salt
> 1¼ cups milk
> Slightly sweetened whipped cream
> Fresh fruit, such as berries or kiwi

1. Preheat oven to 325° F. Wash and dry 14 tin cans, 14 to 16 ounces each, or 14 small (1-cup) soufflé dishes; grease and flour insides.

2. In large bowl of electric mixer, beat butter, sugar, eggs, and vanilla until fluffy. Beat 5 minutes on high speed, scraping bowl occasionally.

3. Combine flour, baking powder, and salt.

4. Add dry ingredients to batter alternately with milk.

5. Spoon about ⅓ cup of batter into each prepared tin can. Bake until a toothpick inserted in center comes out clean, 25 to 30 minutes. (The tops will not brown.)

6. Remove to a wire rack and cool completely, until the edges become dry and crusty. Run a knife around the inside of cans or dishes to loosen edges, tap on a counter, then turn cakes out; they should slide out easily.

7. With a serrated knife, cut off and discard the rounded tops of cakes. Turn cakes upside down so cut edges are on the bottom. Cut cakes into two layers and fill with whipped cream and fresh fruit.

Makes 14.

Timesaver Tip Cake batter can be made ahead and frozen *before* baking. Complete steps 1 through 4 and spoon batter into cans. Wrap cans with heavy-duty aluminum foil. Label and date, and freeze at 0° F up to 6 weeks. To bake, do not thaw. Remove foil and bake at 325° F until cakes test done, about 30 minutes. Complete steps 6 and 7.

AUTUMN APPLE CAKE

Serve this homey cake warm, with Whiskey Sauce (see page 120).

    3 eggs
    ¾ cup vegetable oil
    2 teaspoons vanilla extract
    2¼ cups flour
    1½ cups sugar
    1½ teaspoons ground cinnamon
    ¼ teaspoon ground nutmeg
    ¾ teaspoon baking soda
    ¾ teaspoon baking powder
    ½ teaspoon salt
    3 cups peeled, cored, diced
       apples (about 1½ lbs)
    1½ cups chopped walnuts

1. Preheat oven to 375° F. In large bowl of electric mixer, beat eggs, oil, and vanilla until well combined.

2. Combine flour, sugar, cinnamon, nutmeg, baking soda, baking powder, and salt, stirring to combine thoroughly. Add to egg mixture and stir to blend. Stir in apples and nuts.

3. Spoon batter into a greased 9- by 13-inch baking pan, or a 10-inch fluted or plain tube pan.

4. Bake until a skewer inserted in center comes out clean (30 to 40 minutes, or 40 to 50 minutes if using a tube pan). Cool 30 minutes in pan on rack before cutting.

Serves 12.

Preparation Time About 20 minutes before baking

Timesaver Tip Batter can be made ahead and frozen *before* baking. Line a 9- by 13-inch pan with heavy-duty foil and add batter. Freeze, uncovered, until frozen solid. Remove from pan; wrap tightly. For tube pan, spoon batter into unlined greased pan, wrap pan tightly with heavy-duty aluminum foil, and freeze. Label and date package. Freeze at 0° F up to 4 weeks. To bake, peel off foil; put batter in greased pan. Bake in preheated 375° F oven 35 to 45 minutes, or until pick inserted in center comes out clean. For tube pan, remove foil; bake 40 to 50 minutes.

Step-by-step

FREEZING BATTER

With the frozen batter technique, you can mix up a baked dessert when you've got some time, freeze it for as long as four weeks, then bake it just prior to serving. The quality of the finished dessert will be better than if you froze it after baking.

You simply prepare the batter, freeze it, then bake it directly from the freezer, increasing the baking time as the recipe directs. There's no thawing required.

Package the frozen batter with care. Aluminum foil is an excellent wrapping material; use either heavy-duty foil or a double thickness of regular foil. When wrapping frozen batters, press out as much air as you can and mold the wrapping as close to the food as possible.

Most batters will keep up to four weeks at 0° F. If your freezer doesn't maintain a temperature of 0° F (and many combination refrigerator-freezers don't), keep the batter frozen no more than two weeks.

1. *Pour batter into foil-lined baking pan and smooth the top. Place pan in freezer, uncovered, and freeze until it is solid.*

2. *Remove frozen batter and foil lining. Wrap foil securely around batter, label and date package, and return to freezer. Pan is now free for other uses.*

3. *To bake, grease the baking pan in which the batter was frozen and return the batter to the pan, first peeling away the foil.*

Mix now, bake later: Lemon-Scented Pound Cake, Sour Cream Fudge Cake (page 44), Autumn Apple Cake (page 45), and Baby Cakes (page 44).

LEMON-SCENTED POUND CAKE

A moist, dense cake that's delicious on its own or with fresh fruit, Raspberry Sauce, or Cassis Sauce (both recipes are on page 118).

- 2 cups sugar
- 1 cup butter or margarine, at room temperature
- 2 tablespoons lemon juice
- 2 teaspoons finely grated lemon rind
- 1 teaspoon vanilla extract
- 5 eggs
- 2 cups flour

1. Preheat oven to 350° F. In large bowl of electric mixer, cream together sugar and butter until light and fluffy. Beat in lemon juice, lemon rind, and vanilla.

2. Add eggs in 3 additions, mixing well after each.

3. Sift flour into butter mixture. Mix to blend thoroughly.

4. Spoon batter into greased 10-inch fluted or plain tube pan. Bake until a skewer inserted in center comes out clean (1 hour to 1 hour and 15 minutes). Cool on wire rack 15 to 20 minutes before turning cake out of pan.

Makes 1 cake, 10 to 12 servings.

Preparation Time About 20 minutes before baking

Timesaver Tip Cake batter can be made ahead and frozen *before* baking. Wrap pan tightly with heavy-duty aluminum foil. Label and date. Freeze at 0° F up to 4 weeks. Do not thaw. To bake, remove foil and bake at 350° F until a skewer inserted in center comes out clean (about 1 hour and 15 to 20 minutes). If cake starts to get too brown, cover loosely with aluminum foil the last 30 minutes of baking. Cool on wire rack 15 to 20 minutes before turning out of pan.

RAISIN SCONES

You can make scones in any size or shape you wish—circles, squares, triangles, hearts, crescents, stars. They're delicious as "sandwiches" filled with thinly sliced ham.

   3½ cups flour
   2   tablespoons cream of tartar
   2   teaspoons baking soda
   ½   teaspoon salt
   ⅓   cup sugar
   ¾   cup butter
   ½   cup buttermilk
   2   eggs
   1¼ cups raisins

1. Preheat oven to 375° F. In a large bowl combine flour, cream of tartar, baking soda, salt, and sugar.

2. Cut in butter until mixture resembles fine crumbs.

3. Mix together buttermilk and eggs. Add to dry ingredients, mixing to form a soft dough. Stir in raisins.

4. Knead dough on a floured surface several times.

5. Pat out dough 1 inch thick. Cut into desired shapes and place on ungreased baking sheets.

6. Bake until golden brown (15 to 20 minutes).

Makes 18 to 24.

Preparation Time About 20 minutes, before baking

Timesaver Tip Scones can be made ahead and frozen *before* baking. Place on a baking sheet and freeze, uncovered, until frozen solid. Transfer to freezer bags or wrap in heavy-duty aluminum foil. Label and date package, and freeze at 0° F up to 6 weeks. To bake, do not thaw. Place scones 1½ to 2 inches apart on baking sheets. Bake in a preheated 375° F oven until golden brown (20 to 25 minutes).

PECAN-CORN MUFFINS

Pecans add a crunchy surprise to these buttermilk corn muffins.

   1¼ cups yellow cornmeal
   ¾   cup sugar
   ¾   cup flour
   2   teaspoons baking powder
   ¾   teaspoon baking soda
   ¼   teaspoon salt
   1   cup broken pecans, lightly
       toasted
   1   cup buttermilk
   ⅓   cup butter, melted
   2   eggs

1. Preheat oven to 400° F. In a medium bowl combine cornmeal, sugar, flour, baking powder, baking soda, and salt. Stir in pecans.

2. In another medium bowl mix buttermilk, melted butter, and eggs.

3. By hand, gently stir in dry ingredients just until batter is evenly moistened; do not overmix.

4. Line muffin pans with cupcake liners. Spoon in batter until liners are three-fourths full.

5. Bake until a toothpick inserted in center comes out clean (12 to 15 minutes). Cool muffins on wire racks.

Makes 18.

Preparation Time 15 minutes, before baking

Timesaver Tip Muffin batter may be made ahead and frozen *before* baking. Freeze batter, uncovered, in lined muffin pans until frozen solid. Remove muffins from pan and package in heavy-duty aluminum foil or plastic bags. Label and date, and freeze at 0° F up to 4 weeks. To bake, do not thaw. Return muffins to pans and bake at 375° F until muffins test done, 30 to 35 minutes.

WHITE CHOCOLATE AND MACADAMIA NUT BROWNIES

Not quite your traditional brownie— and absolutely scrumptious!

   ⅔   cup macadamia nuts
   1   cup plus 2 tablespoons flour
   ¾   teaspoon baking powder
   ¼   teaspoon salt
   ¼   cup unsalted butter
   ½   cup sugar
   2   tablespoons water
   9   ounces white chocolate
   2   large eggs
   1   teaspoon vanilla extract

1. Preheat oven to 325° F. If macadamia nuts are salted, blanch in boiling water to cover for 30 seconds to remove salt. Rinse under cold running water and transfer to a baking sheet. Toast in a 325° F oven until golden brown. Let cool, then coarsely chop. If nuts are unsalted, just toast and chop.

2. Combine flour, baking powder, and salt. Set aside.

3. Place butter, sugar, and water in a medium saucepan over low heat. Cut 6 ounces of the white chocolate into large (1- or 2-inch) chunks and the remaining 3 ounces into small (¼-inch to ½-inch) chips.

4. When butter has melted, remove from heat, add the 6 ounces white chocolate chunks and stir until chocolate melts.

5. Beat in eggs and vanilla. Stir in flour mixture until just blended. Stir in the 3 ounces of white chocolate chips and the nuts.

6. Spread batter in a greased 8- or 9-inch square baking pan. Bake 30 to 35 minutes, or until a toothpick inserted in center comes out clean. Cool on a wire rack, then cut into squares.

Makes 12 to 16 brownies.

Preparation Time 15 minutes
before baking

Timesaver Tip Brownie batter can be made ahead and frozen *before* baking. Line an 8- or 9-inch square pan with heavy-duty foil. Spoon batter into pan. Freeze batter, uncovered, until frozen solid. Remove from pan and wrap tightly. Label and date package. Freeze at 0° F up to 4 weeks. To bake, peel foil from batter and place in greased pan. Bake in a preheated 375° F oven until skewer inserted in center comes out clean (40 to 50 minutes).

Microwave Version

Chocolate may be melted in a microwave oven. Place butter and chocolate in a small glass bowl. Microwave on 50% power for 1 minute, stir, then continue microwaving 1 to 3 minutes more. Stir until smooth. Do not overheat or chocolate will scorch around edges and won't blend smoothly. Stir in sugar and water and continue with step 5. Preparation time and timesaver tip same as above.

BIG BATCHES

Big Batches are make-ahead mixes that you can make in large quantities—even double or triple the amount in these recipes. They come in handy on busy days, and they're easy and fun for kids to make.

Homemade mixes offer several advantages over store-bought: They're less expensive, they're lower in salt, and they're additive-free. In the recipes that follow, you have the option of using either butter or shortening. Some cooks prefer butter; however, mixes made with butter must be stored in the freezer. Those made with vegetable shortening can be stored up to 6 months in the cupboard and are lower in cholesterol as well.

CORN BREAD MIX

> 4   cups cornmeal
> 4   cups flour
> ¾   cup sugar
> ¼   cup baking powder
> 2¼ teaspoons salt
> 1   cup butter, margarine,
>   or vegetable shortening

1. In a large bowl combine cornmeal, flour, sugar, baking powder, and salt; stir to blend.

2. Cut in butter with a pastry blender or two knives until mixture resembles fine meal.

3. Store in one large plastic bag or divide into four 2⅓-cup portions. Mix made with butter or margarine can be stored in freezer up to 4 months. Mix made with shortening can be stored in cupboard up to 6 months.

Makes 4 batches.

Preparation Time 10 minutes

Spicy Chili Butter is delicious slathered on hot cornsticks (see Corn Muffins With Chili Butter, page 50). Keep a ready supply of Corn Bread Mix in the freezer to bake as muffins, cornsticks, or corn bread.

With Basic Brownie Mix on hand, you can make brownies on the spur of the moment. Here, Berry's Brownies, made with chopped walnuts, are perfect with a glass of cold milk.

CORN MUFFINS WITH CHILI BUTTER

This batter can be baked either in muffin tins or in cornstick pans.

- 1 cup milk
- 1 egg
- 2⅓ cups Corn Bread Mix (see page 49)

Chili Butter

- ½ cup butter or margarine, at room temperature
- 1 teaspoon lime juice (optional)
- ¼ to ½ teaspoon cayenne pepper
- ¼ to ½ teaspoon ground cumin

1. Preheat oven to 425° F. Beat together milk and egg. Add Corn Bread Mix. Stir just until dry ingredients are moistened—mixture should be lumpy.

2. Grease muffin cups or line with cupcake liners. Spoon mixture into cups, filling two-thirds full.

3. Bake until a pick inserted in center comes out clean (12 to 18 minutes).

4. Serve warm with Chili Butter.

Makes 1 dozen muffins.

Preparation Time About 5 minutes, before baking

Chili Butter Beat butter until light and fluffy. Beat in remaining ingredients. Spoon butter into a crock. Serve at room temperature.

Makes ½ cup.

Preparation Time 5 minutes

OLD-FASHIONED CORN BREAD

The batter can be prepared in the food processor.

- 1 cup milk
- 1 egg
- 2⅓ cups Corn Bread Mix (see page 49)

1. Preheat oven to 425° F. Beat together milk and egg.

2. Add Corn Bread Mix. Stir just until dry ingredients are moistened—mixture should be lumpy.

3. Grease an 8- or 9-inch square baking pan. Spoon in batter. Bake until a toothpick inserted in center comes out clean (about 15 minutes).

4. Cut into squares and serve warm.

Serves 9.

Preparation Time About 5 minutes, before baking

BASIC BROWNIE MIX

- 6 cups sugar
- 4 cups flour
- 2¼ cups unsweetened cocoa
- 2 teaspoons baking powder
- 1 teaspoon salt
- 4 cups butter, margarine, or shortening

1. In a large bowl combine sugar, flour, cocoa, baking powder, and salt. Cut butter in with a pastry blender until mixture resembles cornmeal.

2. Store mix in one large plastic bag or package in 3-cup portions. (Mix should be measured firmly packed.)

3. Mix made with butter or margarine can be stored in freezer up to 4 months. Mix made with shortening can be stored in cupboard up to 6 months.

Makes enough mix for 4 batches of brownies.

Preparation Time 15 minutes

BERRY'S BROWNIES

These are simple, cakey brownies. For a richer brownie, make one of the variations: fold chocolate chips into the batter, or spread the brownies with icing.

   3 *cups Basic Brownie Mix*
   3 *eggs*
 1½ *teaspoons vanilla extract*
  ¾ *cup chopped walnuts*

1. Preheat oven to 350° F. In an 8- or 9-inch square pan, stir together Basic Brownie Mix, eggs, vanilla, and nuts until dry ingredients are well moistened.

2. Bake until a toothpick inserted in the center comes out barely moist, 20 to 25 minutes. Do not overbake.

3. Cool brownies on a wire rack, then cut into squares.

Makes 16 squares.

Preparation Time 5 minutes, before baking

Double Chocolate Brownies Stir 1 package (6 oz) semisweet chocolate chips into the batter.

Quick-Iced Brownies Break up 1 or 2 milk chocolate bars into squares. After removing brownies from oven, place chocolate pieces on top and spread chocolate as it melts.

Microwave Version

1. In an 8- or 9-inch square glass dish, stir together Basic Brownie Mix, eggs, vanilla, and nuts until dry ingredients are well moistened.

2. Shield corners of dish with aluminum foil (see page 40). Microwave on 70% power 10 to 12 minutes, rotating dish, if necessary, for even doneness. Brownies are done when a toothpick inserted in center comes out barely moist. Remove foil shields the last 2 minutes of cooking.

3. Cool brownies on a wire rack, then cut into squares.

COOKIE MIX

   9 *cups flour*
 3¼ *cups brown sugar*
 2½ *cups granulated sugar*
   4 *teaspoons baking soda*
   1 *tablespoon salt*
   4 *cups butter, margarine, or shortening*

1. In a large bowl combine flour, sugars, baking soda, and salt; stir to blend. Cut in butter with a pastry blender or 2 knives until mixture resembles coarse meal.

2. Store mix in one large bag or divide into four 4¾-cup portions. Mix made with butter or margarine can be stored in freezer up to 4 months. Mix made with shortening can be stored in cupboard up to 6 months.

Makes 2 large batches, 6 to 8 dozen cookies.

Preparation Time 10 minutes

CHOCOLATE CHIP COOKIES

Everybody's favorite is easier to make when you start with the Cookie Mix in your pantry.

   2 *eggs*
   1 *teaspoon vanilla extract*
 4¾ *cups Cookie Mix (above)*
   2 *cups (12 oz) chocolate chips*
   1 *cup coarsely chopped nuts (optional)*

1. Preheat oven to 375° F. In a large bowl beat together eggs and vanilla. Add Cookie Mix; beat with electric mixer until smooth. Stir in chips and nuts (if used) by hand.

2. Drop batter by tablespoonfuls onto ungreased baking sheets. Bake until golden brown (8 to 10 minutes). Remove to a wire rack to cool.

Makes 3 to 4 dozen cookies.

Preparation Time 8 to 10 minutes, before baking

COCO-MAC COOKIES

You can also make Coco-Pecan Cookies by substituting chopped toasted pecans for the macadamia nuts.

   2 *eggs*
   1 *teaspoon vanilla extract*
 1¼ *cups coarsely chopped macadamia nuts, toasted (see Note)*
 4¾ *cups Cookie Mix (at left)*
 2¼ *cups flaked or shredded coconut*

1. Preheat oven to 375° F. In a medium bowl beat together eggs and vanilla. Add Cookie Mix; beat with electric mixer until smooth. Stir in macadamia nuts and coconut by hand.

2. Drop tablespoonfuls of batter onto ungreased baking sheets. Bake until golden brown (8 to 12 minutes). Remove cookies to a wire rack to cool.

Makes 4 dozen cookies.

Preparation Time 15 to 20 minutes before baking (add 5 minutes if nuts must be blanched)

Note If macadamia nuts are salted, blanch in boiling water to cover for 30 seconds, to remove salt. Rinse under cold running water and chop coarsely. Transfer to baking sheet and toast in a 325° F oven until golden brown. Set aside to cool. If nuts are unsalted, just chop and toast.

SLEEP-IN PANCAKE MIX

8 *cups flour*
½ *cup sugar*
3 *tablespoons baking powder*
1 *tablespoon baking soda*
2 *teaspoons each salt and
   ground cinnamon*
1 *teaspoon ground nutmeg*
½ *teaspoon ground cloves*

Combine all ingredients in a large bowl. Store in plastic bags or a covered container.

Makes 8 batches of pancakes, about 80 pancakes.

Buckwheat Pancakes Decrease flour by ½ cup and add ½ cup buckwheat flour. Eliminate spices, if desired.

Cornmeal Pancakes Decrease flour by ½ cup and add ½ cup cornmeal. Eliminate spices.

Preparation Time 10 minutes

BUTTERMILK PANCAKES

Use an ice cream scoop to make round pancakes of even size.

1 *cup buttermilk (see Note)*
1 *egg*
2 *tablespoons vegetable oil
   or butter, melted*
1 *cup plus 1 tablespoon Sleep-In
   Pancake Mix (at left)*

1. With a wire whisk or fork, beat buttermilk, egg, and oil until well blended. Add pancake mix; beat until smooth. *Or* use food processor fitted with the steel blade: Put all ingredients in work bowl and pulse four or five times, just to combine ingredients. Do not overprocess.

2. Grease a heated griddle or skillet. To test griddle, sprinkle with a few drops of water. If bubbles skitter around, heat is just right.

3. Ladle batter onto hot griddle. Turn pancakes as soon as they are puffed and full of bubbles but before bubbles break. Bake other side until golden brown.

Makes about 10 pancakes, 4 inches each.

Preparation Time 20 to 25 minutes, including baking

Note Dehydrated buttermilk reconstituted with water is an acceptable substitute for fresh buttermilk.

OVEN PANCAKES

Made by the oven method, the pancakes are ready all at once. A great way to handle an early-morning crowd.

1 *cup buttermilk*
1 *egg*
2 *tablespoons vegetable oil
   or butter, melted*
1 *cup plus 1 tablespoon Sleep-in
   Pancake Mix (at left)*
1 *tablespoon butter or
   margarine*

1. Preheat oven to 450° F. With a wire whisk or fork, beat buttermilk, egg, and oil until well blended. Add pancake mix; beat until smooth. *Or* use food processor fitted with the steel blade: Put all ingredients in work bowl and pulse four or five times, just to combine ingredients. Do not overprocess.

2. Use the butter to generously grease 2 baking sheets. Place briefly in preheated oven, watching to make sure butter doesn't burn.

3. Remove pans from oven. Ladle batter onto hot baking sheets. Bake until browned (9 to 12 minutes). You do not need to turn the pancakes.

Makes 10 to 12 pancakes.

Preparation Time About 15 minutes, including baking

COOKIE-JAR FAVORITES, FASTER

Here are three cookie-jar favorites that are so quick and easy they're like child's play to make—in fact, kids will enjoy preparing them. Scottish Butter Cookies (page 54) offer the speed and simplicity of a bar cookie. You just make the dough, spread it in a pan, and bake. The peanut butter cookies (page 54) have only three ingredients: peanut butter, sugar, and egg—no flour. They sound too simple to be good, but they're the best peanut butter cookies around. And what's great about the Brown Bear Cookies (page 54) is that the dough can be dropped onto cookie sheets and frozen. When the urge hits for warm cookies, just bake a batch right from the freezer. Thawing is not necessary.

Easy favorites are, front to back, Quick and Delicious Peanut Butter Cookies, Scottish Butter Cookies, and Brown Bear Cookies. Recipes are on page 54.

SCOTTISH BUTTER COOKIES

High-quality unsalted butter is essential to this recipe.

> 1 cup unsalted butter
> ⅔ cup sugar
> 2 teaspoons vanilla extract
> 2 cups flour
> ¼ teaspoon salt

1. Preheat oven to 350° F. In large bowl of electric mixer, cream butter, sugar, and vanilla until light and fluffy. Mix in flour and salt.

2. Pat mixture evenly into an ungreased 10- by 15-inch jelly roll pan.

3. Bake until pale in color, but not browned (16 to 18 minutes). Do not overbake. Cool about 5 minutes, then cut into squares while still warm. (Cookies will be thin.)

Makes about 4 dozen cookies.

Preparation Time 10 to 15 minutes, before baking

BROWN BEAR COOKIES

Children love to make and eat this spicy, chewy cookie.

> ¾ cup butter or margarine
> 1 cup sugar
> 1 egg
> ¼ cup light molasses
> 2 cups flour
> 2 teaspoons baking soda
> 1 teaspoon ground cinnamon
> ¾ teaspoon ground ginger
> ¼ teaspoon each *ground cloves and salt*

1. Preheat oven to 375° F. In large bowl of electric mixer, cream butter and sugar until light and fluffy. Mix in egg and molasses.

2. Combine flour, baking soda, cinnamon, ginger, cloves, and salt. Add to butter mixture, mixing thoroughly.

3. Form dough into small balls. Place 1½ to 2 inches apart on greased baking sheets.

4. Bake until done, 10 to 15 minutes. Remove to wire rack to cool.

Makes 2 dozen cookies.

Preparation Time About 10 minutes, before baking

Timesaver Tip Cookie dough can be made ahead and frozen *before* baking. Place balls of dough on baking sheets. Freeze, uncovered, until frozen solid. Package in heavy-duty foil or plastic bags. To bake, place cookies 1½ to 2 inches apart on greased baking sheets. Do not thaw. Bake at 375° F 25 to 35 minutes. Remove from pans immediately. Cool on wire racks.

QUICK AND DELICIOUS PEANUT BUTTER COOKIES

A great peanut butter cookie, and so easy!

> 1 cup peanut butter
> ⅔ cup sugar
> 1 egg

1. Preheat oven to 350° F. In a medium bowl combine peanut butter, sugar, and egg; blend well.

2. Form dough into 1-inch balls. Place 1½ to 2 inches apart on greased baking sheets. Using a fork, press a crisscross pattern into dough.

3. Bake 12 to 15 minutes, or until lightly browned. Cool on wire rack.

Makes about 2 dozen cookies.

Preparation Time 10 to 15 minutes, before baking

SHORTCUT YEAST BREAD BAKING TECHNIQUES

Traditional yeast bread baking is a time-consuming and messy process. You can streamline preparation and save time and cleanup by making use of the food processor, heavy-duty mixer, and/or microwave oven. And you can cut rising time by up to half by using quick-rising active dry yeast, a new product.

Mixing and Kneading

With a food processor you can mix and knead dough in about a minute! It saves on cleanup too. The recipes that follow have been developed for the food processor, and you can adapt just about any yeast bread recipe to this appliance.

You'll need a processor with a strong motor; check the manufacturer's manual to see whether yours can handle yeast doughs. The average processor will hold only enough ingredients for one loaf of bread. If you want to make more, it's best to make consecutive batches, even if you have a larger work bowl.

The recipes that follow call for processing the dry ingredients, including the yeast, just to combine them. Cut in butter or margarine finely; the butter should almost disappear into the flour mixture. Liquid can be added cold—water straight from the tap or milk from the refrigerator. As the processor mixes and kneads, the dough warms sufficiently to start the yeast fermenting.

In using your processor to knead dough, process the dough until it forms a ball, and then for about 60 seconds more. Overprocessing causes the dough to overheat, and the dough may work up under the blade and onto the drive shaft, making quite a mess. Also, you can overtax the processor's motor. However, if you underprocess the dough, the bread will be coarse and flat. The kneaded dough should feel warm but not hot, and it should feel smooth, elastic, and tacky, but not too sticky.

A heavy-duty mixer fitted with a dough hook saves mixing and kneading time, although not nearly as much as a food processor saves. Just about any yeast bread recipe can be adapted to the mixer by following the manufacturer's directions.

Rising

To start the dough rising, shape it into a ball and place it smooth side down in a lightly oiled bowl, then turn the dough around to coat the entire surface. This light coating of oil keeps the dough moist and prevents it from forming a skin that will inhibit the dough's expansion. Cover the bowl with plastic wrap or a damp towel and place it in a warm, draft-free place. Drafts cause dough to rise slowly and unevenly. During rising the yeast continues to grow, giving off carbon dioxide gas that gently and slowly expands the dough. The first rising will take 1 to 1½ hours. Dough rises faster the second and third times.

Dough should rise until it's doubled in size. The ideal temperature is 80° F to 85° F, but dough will rise at 100° F without killing the yeast. Dough rises nicely in a gas oven warmed by a pilot light or in an electric oven that has been turned on at 200° F for 1 minute, then turned off. Create a moist environment in the oven by placing the bowl of dough over a pan of hot water. You can create a warm, moist environment in your microwave oven by microwaving 2 cups of water until the water boils. Turn off the power, set the dough in the microwave oven, and close the door. To save even more on cleanup, you can let dough rise in a plastic

storage bag, which will create a moist, warm environment for the dough. With lightly floured hands, transfer the dough to a lightly floured 1-gallon plastic storage bag. Squeeze out the air and tightly close the bag with a wire twist or rubber band, leaving space for the dough to rise. Set aside in a warm place until the dough has doubled in bulk. The disadvantage to this method is that it is sometimes hard to tell when the dough has doubled in size.

Long, slow rising lets yeast doughs develop their fullest flavor. But when you're in a hurry, there are ways to reduce rising time by about half.

Quick-rising active dry yeast is a new product on the market that cuts rising time by up to half. You can substitute it for active dry yeast in almost any recipe. It's available in foil packets and resealable jars.

A light coat of butter just before baking gives Old-Fashioned Potato Pan Rolls (see page 61) their beautifully browned tops. Make them with either freshly mashed potato or prepared instant potato.

Everyone loves pizza! Start with Pizza Crust and add the most tempting toppings you can imagine. Here, ham, asparagus, and cheese make a light pie.

The micro-rise method is another way to cut rising time by at least half. If your microwave oven can't operate on 10% power (check the operating manual), do not try this method. You will also need a rapid-response thermometer.

To micro-rise one or two standard-size loaves, set a measuring cup of hot water in the back corner of your microwave oven. Place the dough in a large, greased glass bowl and cover with plastic wrap. Microwave it on 10% power 6 to 10 minutes for one loaf, 8 to 12 minutes for two. Check the internal temperature of the dough with a rapid-response thermometer; the temperature should not rise above 100° F. Let the dough rest 10 minutes. Microwave on 10% power for 3 to 5 minutes longer if the dough's internal temperature is still under 100° F. Then let the dough rest in the microwave oven (power off) until it has doubled in size. Punch down and shape. Place the dough in a baking pan and do the second rising. If you bake the dough in a glass dish, you can do the second rising in the microwave oven, too.

The micro-rise method takes some practice. But after experimenting with it a few times, you'll find it a real timesaver. Note that doughs made with quick-rising active dry yeast will not rise any faster by the micro-rise method than will doughs made with regular active dry yeast.

Baking and Storing

For the best volume and texture, preheat the oven before baking yeast breads.

When the bread is done, it should be a beautiful golden color. The most common test for doneness of bread is a hollow sound produced when you tap the crust lightly.

Remove baked bread from the pan immediately and cool it on a wire rack to prevent the bottom from getting soggy. To slice bread, use a serrated knife and a sawing motion.

After the bread is completely cool, store at room temperature, tightly wrapped in plastic wrap or aluminum foil or an airtight plastic bag. Unless you live in an environment of exceptionally high humidity, storing bread in the refrigerator will cause it to dry out more quickly than it will at room temperature. Breads enriched with eggs, butter, and fruit such as raisins keep longer than plain breads because of their higher fat and moisture content. Home-baked yeast breads also freeze beautifully. For instructions on reheating them in the microwave, see page 40.

Freezing Yeast Doughs

Freezing dough allows you to organize your time so that you can prepare the dough and clean up when it's convenient, then bake the bread just before serving. As with frozen batters (see page 43), the quality of yeast baked goods is superior when you freeze the dough rather than the finished product (although you can also freeze the baked bread). Remember, however, that doughs can be frozen for only a short time—3 weeks is the maximum.

To freeze dough, let it complete its first rise, then form it into the desired shape—a loaf or whatever. Coat the dough lightly with oil. Line the baking pan with a layer of heavy-duty aluminum foil topped with plastic wrap. (See page 43 for packaging material for frozen batters.) Place dough in pans and fold plastic wrap loosely over it; freeze until dough is solid. Remove package from pan and wrap tightly, molding the foil close to the dough to prevent air pockets. Label and date package. Freeze at 0° F for up to 3 weeks. If your freezer doesn't maintain a temperature of 0° F (many combination refrigerator-freezers don't), freeze the dough no more than 1 week.

To defrost, remove dough from wrappings. Place in the baking pan in which it was frozen and cover loosely with a damp towel or plastic wrap. Let stand in a warm place until doubled in bulk, from 1½ to 4 hours—time depends on factors such as shape and size of dough and temperature of the room. Bake as directed in the recipe.

PIZZA CRUST

Add fresh vegetables, bits of ham, grated cheese—whatever sounds good—to make a gourmet pizza.

About 3 cups flour
½ cup yellow cornmeal
1 package active dry yeast or quick-rising active dry yeast
1 tablespoon sugar
½ teaspoon salt
1 cup cool water
2 tablespoons olive oil

1. Read "Shortcut Yeast Bread Baking Techniques," pages 54 to this page.

2. In a food processor fitted with a steel blade, process flour, cornmeal, yeast, sugar, and salt just to blend.

3. With motor running, add water in a steady stream. Process until mixture comes away from sides of work bowl. Process 30 seconds to knead dough. If dough is sticky, add more flour and process 30 to 60 seconds longer. Dough should feel tacky, smooth, elastic, and warm but not hot.

4. Remove dough from processor and shape into ball. Place ball in an oiled bowl, turn to coat it with oil, and cover with plastic wrap or a damp towel. Let dough rise until doubled in bulk, 30 to 60 minutes.

5. Punch dough down and divide it in half. Fit each piece into a 12-inch pizza pan. Spread each with toppings of your choice.

Makes two 12-inch pizzas.

Timesaver Tip See "Freezing Yeast Doughs" at left.

MIXING DOUGH IN THE FOOD PROCESSOR

You can adapt almost any yeast bread recipe to the food processor. Be sure your processor can handle yeast doughs. If you want to make more than one loaf at a time, it's best to make consecutive batches, even if you have a larger work bowl.

1. Process the dry ingredients, including the yeast, just to combine them. With on/off pulsing, cut in butter finely; it should almost disappear into the flour mixture.

2. Add the water in a steady stream while the motor runs. Continue processing until the mixture comes away from the sides of the work bowl and starts to form a ball. To knead dough, process about 60 seconds more, being careful not to overwork it.

HOMEMADE HAMBURGER AND HOT DOG BUNS

    4 to 4½ cups flour
    ¼ cup sugar
    1 package active dry yeast or
       quick-rising active dry yeast
    1¼ teaspoons salt
    6 tablespoons butter or marga-
       rine, cut into 6 pieces
    1 cup cool water
    1 egg
       Melted butter and sesame
       seeds (optional)

1. Read "Shortcut Yeast Bread Baking Techniques," pages 54–57. In a food processor fitted with steel blade, process 4 cups flour, sugar, yeast, and salt just to blend. With on/off pulsing, cut in butter finely.

2. In a separate bowl, whisk together water and egg. With processor running, quickly add to yeast mixture. Process until mixture comes away from sides of bowl. Process 30 to 60 seconds to knead dough. If dough is sticky, add more flour and process 15 to 30 seconds longer. Dough should feel tacky, smooth, elastic, and warm but not hot.

3. Remove dough from processor and shape into a ball. Place in an oiled bowl, turn to coat with oil, and cover with plastic wrap or a damp towel. Let rise until doubled in bulk.

4. Punch dough down. Let rest 5 minutes. Divide into 12 pieces. *For hamburger buns:* Flatten each piece into a 5-inch circle; brush with melted butter and sprinkle with seeds, if desired. *For hot dog buns:* Pull each piece out 6 inches long.

5. Place shaped dough on greased baking sheets. Cover with plastic wrap or a damp towel and let rise in a warm place until doubled in bulk, about 30 minutes. Preheat oven to 375° F. Bake until golden (12 to 15 minutes). Remove from baking sheets to cool on wire racks.

Makes 12 buns.

Timesaver Tip See page 57 for instructions on freezing yeast doughs.

ANGEL BISCUITS

This is a light, high-rising biscuit with a wonderful yeasty aroma.

    1 package active dry yeast
    2 tablespoons sugar
    2 tablespoons warm (105° to
       115° F) water
    2 to 2¼ cups flour
    1 teaspoon baking powder
    ¼ teaspoon salt
    3 tablespoons butter or
       margarine, cut into chunks
    ⅔ cup buttermilk

1. In a small bowl mix together yeast, sugar, and water; let proof 10 to 15 minutes. In food processor fitted with steel blade, combine 2 cups flour, baking powder, and salt. With on/off pulsing, cut in butter. With motor off, quickly add yeast mixture and buttermilk; process until dough pulls away from sides of bowl. Add more flour if dough is sticky.

2. Turn dough out onto a lightly floured board. Pat out ¼ inch thick; cut with 2- or 2½-inch biscuit cutter. Arrange, barely touching, on greased baking sheet. Prick tops with a fork. Cover pan with plastic wrap. Let rise in a warm place until doubled, about 30 to 40 minutes.

3. Preheat oven to 425° F. Bake until golden brown (10 to 15 minutes).

Makes 10 to 12 biscuits.

Timesaver Tip See page 57 for instructions on freezing yeast doughs.

Micro-Rise Method Preheat oven to 425° F. Complete step 1. Cut biscuits as directed in step 2. Arrange biscuits, barely touching, in a lightly greased round glass baking dish; cover loosely with plastic wrap. Place measuring cup of warm water in back corner of microwave oven and biscuits in center of oven. Microwave on 10% power about 4 to 5 minutes. Let rest 5 minutes at room temperature, or until doubled in bulk. Bake as directed in step 3.

WHOLE WHEAT LOAVES

To make two loaves, double the recipe, processing in two batches.

- 2½ to 2¾ cups all-purpose or bread flour
- 1½ cups whole wheat flour
- ¼ cup firmly packed brown sugar
- 1 package active dry yeast or quick-rising active dry yeast
- 1 teaspoon salt
- 3 tablespoons butter or margarine, cut into 3 pieces
- 1½ cups cool water

1. Read "Shortcut Yeast Bread Baking Techniques," pages 54–57.

2. In a food processor fitted with a steel blade, process 2½ cups all-purpose or bread flour, whole wheat flour, brown sugar, yeast, and salt just to blend. With on/off pulsing, cut in butter finely, until it almost disappears.

3. With motor running, add water quickly. Process until the mixture comes away from the sides of bowl. Process 30 seconds to knead dough. If dough is sticky, add more all-purpose or bread flour and process 15 to 30 seconds longer. Dough should feel tacky, smooth, elastic, and warm but not hot.

4. Remove dough from processor and shape into a ball. Place in oiled bowl, turn to coat with oil, and cover with plastic wrap or a damp towel. Let rise until doubled in bulk.

5. Punch dough down. Let rest 5 minutes. Form into a loaf. Place in a greased 9- by 5-inch bread pan. Cover with plastic wrap or a damp towel; let rise until doubled in bulk.

6. Preheat oven to 375° F. With a sharp knife, make 3 or 4 diagonal slashes in top of loaf, ¼ to ½ inch deep. Bake until well browned (40 to 50 minutes). When bread is done, loaf will sound hollow when tapped. Immediately remove loaf from pan; cool on a wire rack.

Makes 1 loaf.

Timesaver Tip See page 57 for instructions on freezing yeast doughs.

Sweetened with brown sugar, Whole Wheat Loaves are the kind of wholesome home-baked bread everyone loves. A food processor makes quick work of the usually time-consuming task of mixing and kneading the dough.

The food processor speeds preparation of Brioche Bread dough, which may be baked in the traditional topknot form, as a large loaf, or in small loaf pans.

OLD-FASHIONED POTATO PAN ROLLS

Here's a fast way to make absolutely delicious golden pan rolls!

    3¼ to 3¾ cups all-purpose
        or bread flour
    1 package active dry yeast or
        quick-rising active dry yeast
    ¼ cup sugar
    ½ teaspoon salt
    6 tablespoons cold butter or
        margarine, cut into chunks
    ½ cup freshly mashed or
        prepared instant potato
    ¾ cup milk
    1 egg
        Melted butter

1. Read "Shortcut Yeast Bread Baking Techniques," pages 54-57.

2. In a food processor fitted with a steel blade, process 3¼ cups flour, the yeast, sugar, and salt just to blend. With on/off pulsing, cut in butter finely, until it almost disappears.

3. In a separate bowl, mix together mashed potato, milk, and egg. With processor motor running, quickly add potato mixture to yeast mixture. Process until mixture comes away from the side of the bowl.

4. Process 30 seconds to knead dough. If dough is sticky, add more flour and process 15 to 30 seconds longer. Dough should feel tacky, smooth, elastic, and warm but not hot.

5. Remove dough from processor and shape into a ball. Place ball in an oiled bowl, turn to cover it with oil, and cover bowl with plastic wrap or a damp towel. Let dough rise until doubled in bulk.

6. Punch dough down. Let rest 5 minutes. Divide dough into 24 pieces (approximately 1¼ ounces each). Shape each piece into a ball, tucking the edges under to draw the surface of the dough tight. Arrange the dough in 2 round cake or pie pans. Cover loosely with plastic wrap or a damp towel and let rise until doubled in bulk.

7. Preheat oven to 375° F. Brush tops with melted butter. Bake until golden brown (20 to 30 minutes). Remove from pan to cool on a wire rack. Brush tops again with melted butter.

Makes 2 dozen rolls.

Timesaver Tip See page 57 for instructions on freezing yeast doughs.

BRIOCHE BREAD

A rich bread that is easy to make and beautifully yellow and buttery. It's excellent for toast and sandwiches. If you have tiny (approximately 3½- by 1½-inch) loaf pans, the brioche can be shaped and served as individual loaves. The recipe will make 8 to 10 of these little loaves, which will bake in about 30 minutes.

    3 to 3½ cups all-purpose
        or bread flour
    ¼ cup sugar
    1¼ teaspoons salt
    1 package active dry yeast or
        quick-rising active dry yeast
    12 tablespoons cold butter,
        cut into 12 pieces
    ½ cup milk
    4 large eggs
    1 teaspoon water

1. Read "Shortcut Yeast Bread Baking Techniques," pages 54-57.

2. In a food processor fitted with a steel blade, process 3 cups flour, the sugar, salt, and yeast just to blend. With on/off pulsing, cut in butter finely.

3. In a large measuring cup, whisk together milk and 3 eggs. With processor motor running, add the liquid quickly to the yeast mixture. Process until mixture comes away from sides of bowl.

4. Process about 30 seconds to knead dough. If dough is sticky, add more flour and process about 30 seconds longer. Dough should feel tacky, smooth, elastic, and warm but not hot.

5. Remove dough from processor and shape into a ball. Place ball in an oiled bowl, turn to coat it with oil, and cover with plastic wrap or a damp towel. Let dough rise until doubled in bulk.

6. Punch dough down. Let rest 5 minutes. Form dough into a loaf. Place in a buttered 9- by 5-inch loaf pan or two 6- by 3-inch pans. Cover dough with a damp towel or plastic wrap. Let rise in pan until doubled in bulk.

7. Preheat oven to 350° F. Brush top with glaze made by beating together remaining egg and the water. Bake until golden brown—45 to 50 minutes for 1 loaf, 30 to 40 minutes for 2. Immediately remove from pan and cool on a wire rack.

Makes 1 large or 2 small loaves.

Timesaver Tip See page 57 for instructions on freezing yeast doughs.

SLEEP-IN SUNDAY BRUNCH

Warm Sauté of Citrus Fruits With Lemon-Honey Crème Fraîche

Favorite Sour Cream Coffee Cake

Scrambled Eggs

Coffee

It's fun to entertain at brunch—but not to get up early to prepare the food. This menu lets you sleep in and still offer guests a homemade meal. Make the coffee cake batter ahead, freeze it, then bake it directly from the freezer. While it bakes, prepare the fruit sauté and top it with crème fraîche chilled overnight in the refrigerator. Make the coffee, scramble the eggs, and Sunday brunch is on the table.

WARM SAUTÉ OF CITRUS FRUITS WITH LEMON-HONEY CRÈME FRAÎCHE

Glowing with color, this is a refreshing and festive dish for a brunch. The fruity tartness contrasts nicely with a smooth crème fraîche.

- 2 tangelos or oranges
- 1 tangerine
  Half a grapefruit
- 2 tablespoons butter or margarine
- 1 tablespoon honey
- 1 cup sliced strawberries
  Mint leaves, for garnish (optional)

Lemon-Honey Crème Fraîche

- ½ cup whipping cream (not ultrapasteurized)
- 1 tablespoon lemon juice
- 1½ teaspoons honey
- 1 teaspoon finely grated lemon rind

1. Prepare Lemon-Honey Crème Fraîche.

2. Finely grate 1½ teaspoons tangelo rind. Squeeze juice from same fruit.

3. Peel and separate segments of remaining tangelo, tangerine, and grapefruit.

4. Melt butter in a large skillet. Stir in honey, tangelo rind, and tangelo juice. Bring to a boil. Boil, stirring constantly, until reduced by half.

5. Add citrus fruits. Cook, basting with sauce, just until heated through; do not overcook. Remove from heat and stir in strawberries.

6. Serve fruit in shallow bowls or on small plates. Garnish with mint, if desired. Pass crème fraîche at table.

Serves 4.

Preparation Time About 20 minutes

Lemon-Honey Crème Fraîche In a small bowl stir together cream, lemon juice, honey, and lemon rind.

Cover and let mixture stand at room temperature 3 to 6 hours or overnight. It will thicken slightly. Crème Fraîche can be stored, covered, in the refrigerator; this will thicken it more.

Makes ½ cup.

Microwave Version Complete steps 1 through 3. Put butter in glass dish; microwave on 100% power until it melts. Stir in honey, tangelo rind, and tangelo juice. Microwave on 100% power 4 to 6 minutes, until reduced by half, stirring once. Add fruits; microwave on 100% power 1 to 3 minutes, just until heated through, stirring after 1 minute. Do not overcook. Stir in strawberries. Serve as directed in step 6.

FAVORITE SOUR CREAM COFFEE CAKE

A cinnamon and nut mixture serves as both filling and topping for this quick and easy breakfast or brunch cake.

- 1 cup butter or margarine, at room temperature
- 1¼ cups sugar
- 2 eggs
- 1 cup sour cream
- 1½ teaspoons vanilla extract
- 2 cups flour
- 1 teaspoon baking powder
- ½ teaspoon baking soda
- ¼ teaspoon salt

Topping

- 1¼ cups broken pecans or walnuts
- ¼ cup sugar
- 1 tablespoon ground cinnamon

1. Preheat oven to 350° F. Butter a 9-inch fluted or plain tube pan.

2. In large bowl of electric mixer, cream butter and sugar until light and fluffy. Beat in eggs, sour cream, and vanilla.

3. Stir together flour, baking powder, baking soda, and salt. Gradually beat into butter mixture.

4. Prepare topping. Scatter half the topping evenly over bottom of pan. Spoon in half the batter. Add remaining topping and spoon on remaining batter.

5. Bake 50 to 60 minutes, or until toothpick inserted in center comes out clean. Cool 15 minutes before removing from pan.

Makes one 9-inch coffee cake, 8 to 12 servings.

Preparation Time About 20 minutes, before baking

Topping In a small bowl, combine nuts, sugar, and cinnamon.

Timesaver Tip Coffee cake may be made ahead and frozen *before* baking. Wrap tube pan tightly with heavy-duty aluminum foil, label and date, and freeze at 0° F up to 6 weeks. To bake, do not thaw. Remove foil and bake at 350° F until cake tests done, about 1 hour. Cool 15 minutes before removing from pan.

Favorite Sour Cream Coffee Cake, Warm Sauté of Citrus Fruits With Lemon-Honey Crème Fraîche, and scrambled eggs make up an easy menu for Sunday brunch. Add a steaming pot of coffee, and enjoy a relaxed meal with friends.

For a no-fuss dinner, start with top-quality food—such as fresh fish and shellfish—that can be prepared simply and served with little embellishment.

Dinner, Quick & Easy

Dinner-in-a-hurry doesn't have to mean hot dogs or yet another frozen entrée. In this chapter you'll find recipes for main dishes, both plain and fancy, that can be prepared quickly. They include fish and shellfish, perfect for microwaving (pages 66–68); sautéed, grilled, broiled, and baked entrées (pages 70–75); plus a selection of seasoned butters for quick, light saucing. There are also recipes for hearty main dishes (pages 77–78) to make in double batches so you can freeze half, and a generous assortment of pasta sauces that freeze well, ready to heat up for a homemade dinner-in-a-hurry (pages 80–83).

Cooking fish fillets in parchment with a tangy mix of orange and lemon rinds and juices makes a quick, low-calorie en-trée. The taste-tempting dish cooks speedily in the microwave oven, and the parchment means no pan to clean.

MICROWAVED FISH AND SHELLFISH

An important component of many contemporary diets, fish and shellfish are particularly suited to timesaver cooking. They are ideal for the microwave oven—all the recipes that follow call for microwave cooking. In addition, fish and shellfish provide protein without high caloric content. Since they combine well with simple flavorings and sauces, they can be a major part of an eating plan that emphasizes light meals.

CITRUS-SCENTED FILLETS EN PAPILLOTE

Cooking in parchment paper is both practical and attractive. The paper encases the fish fillets, assuring flavor by sealing in natural juices and flavorings and easing cleanup as well. The presentation is fun because you cut open the papillotes at the table and eat right from the paper. See the step-by-step sequence at right for instructions on preparing the fish in parchment.

4 skinless, thin, lean white fish
fillets (5 to 6 oz each) such as
sole, flounder, or pompano
Salt and white pepper to taste
2 tablespoons butter or
margarine
Grated rind and juice of half
a large orange, remaining
half cut into 4 wedges, for
garnish
Grated rind and juice of half
a lemon, remaining half cut
into 4 wedges, for garnish
2 tablespoons finely chopped
chives or green onion tops

1. Cut 4 pieces of parchment paper or foil into rough heart shapes measuring about 12 inches long and 10 inches at widest point. Paper must be at least 3 inches longer than fish.

2. Butter paper. Rinse fillets; pat dry with paper towels. Season with salt and pepper. Place 1 fillet on right side of each heart, thickest end of fillet toward rounded edge of heart.

3. In a small dish, melt butter in microwave oven on 100% power for 30 seconds. Stir grated rinds and juices into melted butter. Drizzle butter mixture over fillets and sprinkle with chives.

4. Fold left half of each heart over fish, matching edges. Starting at top of heart, seal packets by folding edge in 2 or 3 narrow folds. Twist tip of heart to hold case closed.

5. Place papillotes in microwave oven in a spoke pattern, with twisted tips pointing inward. Microwave on 100% power 5 minutes.

6. To serve, place 1 packet on each of 4 serving plates. At the table, cut packets open by slashing a large X on top of each; fold back paper. Place a lemon and orange wedge on each plate.

Serves 4.

Preparation Time About 30 minutes

Step·by·step

COOKING FISH IN PARCHMENT

Cooking in parchment is a popular technique that has a number of advantages. First, it replaces the cooking pan, so it reduces cleanup. Second, very little fat is required. And third, eating the dish becomes a mini-drama: the parchment packet, puffed from expanding air, comes direct from the oven to the table, where it is cut open, releasing a cloud of fragrant steam.

Kitchen parchment is available in some supermarkets and in specialty kitchen supply stores. If necessary, aluminum foil can be substituted for the parchment.

1. Cut sheet of parchment in a rough heart shape, at least 3 inches bigger all around than the fish fillet, and butter it. Place fish fillet on parchment with thickest portion of fillet on the widest part of the parchment.

2. Season fillets with salt and pepper; add mixture of butter and citrus juices and rinds. Bring edges of parchment together and fold over several times, leaving some airspace above the fillet. Twist end of parchment so that packet will stay shut.

MUSSELS ÉTIENNE

Mussels are a delicious and reasonably priced shellfish. Although some are harvested wild off the Atlantic and Pacific coasts, increasing numbers are being farmed. There are also sweet, succulent New Zealand mussels. Cook mussels the day they're purchased. To hold them, cover with a damp towel and refrigerate; do not put them in fresh water.

  4 to 5 dozen mussels
  2 tablespoons butter or
     margarine
  ¼ cup finely chopped shallots
     or onion
  1 clove garlic, minced
  1 teaspoon finely chopped
     fresh thyme or ¼ to ½
     teaspoon dried
  1 teaspoon finely grated orange
     or lemon rind
  1 cup dry white wine
  ½ cup water

1. Scrub mussels with a brush; rinse well. Remove beards (see Note). Check mussels for edibility; live ones will have tightly closed shells or will close their shells when tapped. Discard any that remain open.

2. In a large microwave-proof bowl, microwave butter on 100% power until it melts, about 40 seconds. Add shallots and garlic. Microwave on 100% power 45 seconds.

3. Add thyme, orange rind, wine, and the water. Cover and microwave on 100% power until liquid boils, about 5 to 6 minutes.

4. Add mussels. Cover bowl with plastic wrap. Microwave at 100% power until mussels open, 3 to 5 minutes. Stir mussels with a large spoon after 2 minutes.

5. Use a slotted spoon to remove mussels to individual shallow bowls. Discard any that do not open.

6. If broth is sandy, strain through several layers of cheesecloth. Pour over cooked mussels and serve.

Serves 3 to 5.

Preparation Time 30 minutes

Note Mussels anchor themselves to rocks and pilings with a bundle of tough fibers called beards. De-beard them by grasping the fibers and removing them with a tug.

CREAMY DILL SALMON

Serve these microwaved salmon fillets or steaks with parsleyed rice, a fresh vegetable, and chilled white wine.

  4 salmon fillets (5 to 6 oz
     each) or 4 salmon steaks
     (6 to 8 oz each)
     Salt and freshly ground
     pepper to taste
  2 tablespoons butter or
     margarine
  2 to 3 teaspoons finely chopped
     fresh dill or ½ teaspoon dried,
     or to taste
  1 tablespoon lemon juice,
     or more to taste
  ¼ cup whipping cream
     Dill or parsley sprigs,
     for garnish

1. Gently rinse salmon; remove any small bones with tweezers or needle-nose pliers. Pat dry with paper towels. Season with salt and pepper.

2. Place butter in an 8- or 9-inch square glass baking dish. Microwave on 100% power about 45 seconds to melt butter. Stir dill and lemon juice into butter.

3. Arrange fish in a single layer in baking dish, with the thickest portions toward the outside of the dish. Turn to coat both sides with butter. Cover dish with waxed paper.

4. Microwave on 100% power until fish turns from transparent to opaque, 3 to 6 minutes; give dish a quarter turn after 2 minutes. Check doneness by cutting into center of thickest portion. Place cooked fish on a platter; cover with foil.

5. Stir cream into juices in dish. Microwave on 100% power about 2 minutes. Add salmon juices that have accumulated on dish and microwave 2 to 4 minutes longer, or until sauce thickens and lightly coats a spoon. Season with salt and pepper; adjust dill and lemon juice to taste.

6. Spoon sauce over fish. Garnish with dill or parsley.

Serves 4.

Preparation Time About 20 minutes

LIME-GINGER CRAB

A beautifully colored dish (shown on the cover). You can use the food processor to grate the ginger, mince the garlic, and cut up the carrots and green onions.

  3 tablespoons butter or
     margarine
  2 to 3 teaspoons finely grated
     fresh ginger
  2 to 3 teaspoons minced garlic
  ¼ pound carrots, pared and
     cut into 2-inch matchstick
     pieces (about 1¼ cups)
  3 ounces snow peas, strings
     removed, cut diagonally
     (to make about 1 cup)
  3 green onions, cut into
     2-inch-long strips
  ¾ pound fresh crabmeat or
     frozen crabmeat, thawed
  1 to 2 tablespoons lime juice
     Salt and freshly ground
     pepper to taste

1. In a microwave-proof serving dish, microwave butter on 100% power to melt, about 30 seconds. Add ginger and garlic; microwave on 100% power 20 seconds.

2. Add carrots and microwave about 30 seconds. Stir in snow peas and microwave 30 seconds. Add onion and crabmeat; microwave to heat through, 30 to 60 seconds.

3. Season to taste with lime juice, salt (if necessary), and pepper. Serve immediately.

Serves 4.

Preparation Time About 20 minutes

Temp Probe Cooking

Mussels Étienne cook to perfection in the microwave oven, bathed in a broth of white wine flavored with garlic, citrus rind, and thyme.

TOP-OF-THE-STOVE SUPPERS

One of the timesaver cook's best friends is the sauté pan. Utilizing a film of fat and medium-high heat, sautéing cooks foods quickly, sealing in juices and producing a delectable lightly browned exterior. In addition, sauces can be made right in the pan, reducing the number of dishes to clean up later.

BREAST OF TURKEY WITH MUSTARD-CAPER SAUCE

Turkey breast slices are available in most major supermarkets, but you can cut up your own if they're not. To cut slices, bone a turkey breast and chill or partially freeze the meat to firm it up. With a well-sharpened knife, cut very thin slices across the grain.

> 1 to 1¼ pounds turkey breast
>   slices (8 slices)
>   Salt and freshly ground
>   pepper to taste
> 2 tablespoons butter or
>   margarine
> ½ cup dry vermouth or dry
>   white wine
> ½ cup whipping cream
> 2 teaspoons Dijon mustard
> 1 to 1½ tablespoons drained
>   capers

1. Season turkey slices lightly with salt and pepper. In 2 large skillets over medium heat, melt butter (or melt 1 tablespoon butter in a single skillet and cook half the slices at a time, using second tablespoon of butter for second half of slices).

2. Sauté breasts over medium-high heat 1 to 2 minutes per side; do not overcook. Remove slices to a warmed plate; cover plate with foil to keep warm.

3. Add vermouth to pan. Boil, stirring frequently, until liquid is reduced by half.

4. Stir in cream, mustard, capers, and any turkey juices that have collected on the plate. Boil sauce, stirring constantly, until it has reduced a bit and thickens enough to coat a spoon.

5. Spoon sauce over slices and serve immediately.

Serves 4.

Preparation Time 12 to 15 minutes

SAUSAGE, PEPPERS, AND ONIONS

Serve this hearty skillet dish with thick slices of crusty bread or with pasta. The color is beautiful when you use red bell peppers, but you can substitute green peppers if red ones are not available.

> 1 pound sweet or hot fresh
>   Italian sausage, cut
>   into 1-inch pieces
> 1 small onion or half a large
>   onion, thinly sliced crosswise
>   and separated into rings
> 1 large red bell pepper,
>   cored, seeded, and cut
>   into thin strips
> 2 large cloves garlic, finely
>   chopped
> ½ cup dry vermouth or dry
>   white wine
>   Finely chopped parsley
>   or other fresh herbs (optional)

1. In a large skillet or sauté pan over medium heat, brown sausage until it is cooked through. Remove from pan; set aside.

2. Pour all but 1 tablespoon of fat from pan. Add onions to pan and cook over medium-high heat 1 to 2 minutes. Add pepper and garlic and cook a minute or two more.

3. Return sausage to pan; add vermouth. Cook over high heat, stirring constantly, until wine is reduced by about half. Remove from heat and quickly stir in parsley or other herbs, if used. Serve immediately.

Serves 4.

Preparation Time About 15 minutes

PORK WITH APPLES AND TOASTED WALNUTS

The key to cooking pork is not to overcook it. Although it must be thoroughly done, you need only cook it till the juices run clear, with no pink coloration (an internal temperature of 165° F), which means the chops will still be juicy and flavorful.

> ½ cup broken walnut pieces
> 4 loin pork chops, each
>   1 inch thick
>   Salt and freshly ground
>   pepper
> ⅓ cup apple juice
> 2 tablespoons brandy
> 1 clove garlic, minced
> ¾ teaspoon finely chopped fresh
>   thyme, or ¼ teaspoon dried
> ½ pound (1 large or 2 very
>   small) tart green apples, such
>   as pippin or Granny Smith,
>   cored and sliced ¼ inch thick
>   (leave unpeeled)

1. In a large, heavy skillet over high heat, toast walnuts 2 to 3 minutes, stirring frequently. Remove and set aside.

2. Season chops with salt and pepper to taste. Trim a piece of fat from the edge of one chop. In the same skillet over medium-high heat, heat fat until lightly browned, using a spoon to press and rub fat over bottom of skillet to grease it well. Discard fat and increase heat to high.

3. Add chops; brown quickly on both sides. Pour excess fat, if any, from skillet.

4. Add apple juice, brandy, garlic, thyme, and apples to pan.

5. Cover pan and cook over medium-low heat 5 to 8 minutes. To test for doneness, cut into a chop; it should be tender, juicy, and slightly pink. If pork is done and apples are still crunchy, remove pork to a platter and cover with foil to keep warm. Continue to cook apples until they are tender.

6. Stir walnuts into sauce in pan. Pour walnut-apple sauce over chops. Serve chops immediately.

Serves 4.

Preparation Time 20 to 25 minutes

Apples in two forms—juice and sliced fresh fruit—and crunchy walnuts imbue succulent pork chops with the flavors of autumn. This hearty main dish cooks quickly in the sauté pan.

The food processor mixes up the tart Mint Vinaigrette that tops these lamb chops, broiled just to a juicy medium-rare.

SCALLOPS CHARLOTTE

This is a lovely dish for entertaining. You can use the food processor to chop the chives (or parsley) and shallots (or onions) and to slice the mushrooms.

> 1½ pounds scallops
> 2 tablespoons butter or margarine
> 2 tablespoons finely chopped shallots or onion
> ½ pound small mushrooms, sliced
> ¾ cup whipping cream
> 3 to 4 tablespoons Marsala wine
> Salt and freshly ground white pepper to taste
> Finely chopped chives or parsley, for garnish

1. If you are using large sea scallops, cut them in half horizontally. If you have tiny bay scallops, they can be left whole.

2. In a large skillet over medium heat, melt 1 tablespoon of the butter. Add shallots and mushrooms; sauté over medium-high heat for 2 minutes. Remove to a bowl and set aside.

3. Melt remaining butter in skillet. Add scallops. Sauté 2 to 3 minutes, until scallops are opaque. Using a slotted spoon, remove scallops from skillet and add them to mushroom mixture; set aside.

4. Add cream and wine to liquid in skillet. Add any juices that have accumulated in bowl of scallops.

5. Cook, stirring constantly, over medium heat until sauce reduces to ⅔ to ¾ cup and thickens enough to lightly coat a spoon.

6. Add mushroom and scallop mixture; cook to heat through. Season to taste with salt and pepper. Serve garnished with chives.

Serves 5 to 6.

Preparation Time About 20 minutes

FROM THE OVEN, GRILL, AND BROILER

With careful selection of recipes, the oven, grill, and broiler can contribute to the timesaver cook's repertoire. Choose quick-cooking cuts of meat, let marination shorten the cooking time (see Mexican Steak, page 74), or try a speedy pilaf (see Rice and Lentil Pilaf, page 74). These techniques also lend themselves to low-fat cooking.

LAMB WITH MINT VINAIGRETTE

Mint and lamb are a classic combination. Here is an updated version in which a tart mint sauce sets off broiled lamb chops.

> 1 cup firmly packed mint leaves
> 1 cup firmly packed parsley leaves
> ⅓ cup olive oil
> ¼ cup red or white wine vinegar
> 1 to 2 teaspoons sugar, to taste
> Salt to taste
> 4 lamb chops, each 1 inch thick
> Freshly ground pepper to taste

1. Preheat broiler. Put mint, parsley, oil, vinegar, and sugar into a blender or food processor and process until mixture is smooth and thickened. Adjust sugar, if desired, and season to taste with salt.

2. Trim excess fat from lamb. Broil 2 to 4 minutes per side for medium-rare. (You can also cook the chops on top of the stove. Heat a large, heavy skillet rubbed with some of the fat from chops. Add chops and cook, over medium-high heat, 2 to 4 minutes for medium-rare; turn chops once.) Season chops lightly with salt and pepper.

3. Serve sauce over and to the side of lamb, or pass sauce at table.

Serves 4.

Preparation Time About 20 minutes

GRILLED VEAL WITH LEMON AND HERBS

Veal cooked this way is delicate, lean, delicious, and very quick to prepare.

> Olive or vegetable oil
> Salt and freshly ground pepper to taste
> 4 veal steaks (5 to 6 oz each—see Note)
> 2 tablespoons any combination of the following fresh herbs: parsley, chives, tarragon, mint, basil, and sage, or 2 tablespoons finely chopped parsley
> 4 lemon wedges

1. Lightly brush grill with oil and heat grill very hot. (If you can't grill the veal, you can use a cast-iron skillet, cooking half at a time.)

2. Rub all sides of veal lightly with oil and season to taste with salt and pepper.

3. Grill meat quickly, about 30 to 35 seconds per side.

4. Place veal on warmed plate. Sprinkle with herbs and serve with lemon.

Serves 4.

Preparation Time 5 to 10 minutes

Note If possible, purchase veal sliced ¼ inch thick. If you have thicker cuts, place them between sheets of wax paper; pound with a flat mallet until no thicker than ¼ inch.

RICE AND LENTIL PILAF

This vegetarian main dish requires only 20 minutes to bake. Toss leftovers with a vinaigrette (see page 99) for a delicious salad.

> 2½ cups homemade chicken stock or 2 cans (10½ oz each) chicken broth, preferably low-sodium
> ½ cup raisins
> 1½ tablespoons butter or margarine
> 1½ tablespoons oil
> Half a large onion, diced
> ¾ cup long-grain rice
> ½ cup dried lentils
> ⅛ teaspoon each ground cardamom, ground cinnamon, ground cloves, ground coriander, ground cumin, and ground black pepper
> ¼ pound fresh green beans, cleaned and trimmed to 1-inch lengths
> 1 small baking potato
> ½ cup frozen tiny peas
> 1 carrot, peeled and diced (about 1 cup)
> Half a red or green bell pepper, diced (about ½ cup)
> Chopped cilantro, for garnish

1. Preheat oven to 375° F. In large saucepan over medium heat, combine chicken stock and raisins and bring to a boil. Remove from heat and keep warm.

2. In large Dutch oven or ovenproof casserole over medium-high heat, melt butter and oil. Add onions and sauté until lightly browned.

3. Stir in rice, lentils, cardamom, cinnamon, cloves, coriander, cumin, and pepper. Stir and cook 2 to 3 minutes.

4. Add green beans, potato, peas, carrot, and bell pepper; pour in stock and raisins.

5. Cover and bake until all liquid has been absorbed, about 20 minutes. Serve garnished with chopped cilantro.

Serves 5 to 6.

Preparation Time About 40 minutes

Timesaver Tip Vegetables can be cleaned and cut ahead.

Microwave Version

1. In 3-quart casserole or mixing bowl, combine butter and oil and microwave on 100% power until butter melts, about 45 seconds. Add onion and microwave on 100% power 2 minutes.

2. On top of stove, bring broth and raisins to a boil. Add to casserole along with rice, lentils, spices, and vegetables.

3. Cover and microwave at 100% power for about 10 minutes. Reduce power to 50% and microwave another 12 to 18 minutes, until all liquid has been absorbed. Serve garnished with chopped cilantro. Preparation time about 45 minutes.

MEXICAN STEAK

You can use any cut of beef suitable for broiling or barbecuing, such as the triangle tip of the bottom sirloin, often called a coulotte steak. Prepare the marinade in the morning and let the steaks marinate all day.

> 4 steaks, 4 to 6 ounces each, trimmed of extra fat
> 1 bottle (12 oz) Mexican dark beer
> ½ teaspoon crushed dried red pepper flakes
> 4 cloves garlic, minced
> 1 teaspoon ground cumin
> 1 teaspoon chili powder
> Salt and freshly ground black pepper
> Ancho Chile Butter (optional, see opposite page)

1. With a large meat fork, puncture holes in both sides of steaks; place them in a shallow casserole.

2. Combine beer, red pepper, garlic, cumin, and chili powder to form a marinade; pour over beef. Marinate for 1 to 2 hours at cool room temperature, or longer in the refrigerator.

3. Preheat broiler. Remove meat from marinade and place on rack of broiler pan. Season both sides with salt and pepper to taste. Broil to desired doneness (time will depend on thickness of beef). If desired, serve with a spoonful of Ancho Chile Butter on top of each steak.

Serves 4.

Preparation Time 15 minutes

BROILED CHICKEN BREASTS WITH SEASONED BUTTERS

Simple broiled chicken becomes tantalizingly different with the addition of a flavored butter, a quick way to vary a dinner basic.

> 2 chicken breasts, boned and halved
> Salt and freshly ground black pepper to taste
> Green Onion and Cilantro Butter (see page 76) or Sun-Dried Tomato Butter (see opposite page)

1. Preheat broiler. Season both sides of chicken with salt and pepper.

2. Spread a thin layer of seasoned butter (about ½ teaspoon) on chicken pieces. Place on broiler skin side up and broil until skin turns brown, about 4 minutes. Turn and broil second side. Continue broiling and turning until meat feels slightly firm to the touch and has turned from translucent to opaque. Remove from broiler.

3. Cut ½-inch-deep slashes across skin side of breast. Spoon additional seasoned butter (about 1 teaspoon) on each breast. Serve immediately.

Serves 4.

Preparation Time About 15 minutes

SEASONED BUTTERS

Blending butter with savory flavorings seems to intensify them and artfully blends their colors as well. Seasoned butters make an excellent topping for any roasted, broiled, or barbecued meat, poultry, or fish. The butters can be made up to four days ahead and refrigerated up to a week; they can also be frozen two to three months.

Microwave Version for All Seasoned Butters

Complete step 1. Put butter in a glass dish and microwave on 100% power until butter is melted, about 45 to 60 seconds. Continue with steps 2 and 3.

Sun-Dried Tomato Butter

> 1 ounce (2 to 3 tomato halves)
> sun-dried tomatoes
> ½ cup butter

1. In a food processor or blender, process tomatoes until they are finely chopped.

2. In a small saucepan over medium-high heat, melt butter. With machine running, add hot butter to tomatoes in a fine stream. Blend until color is homogeneous and tomatoes are nearly a paste.

3. Let stand at room temperature until butter reaches a spoonable consistency. Use immediately, or refrigerate or freeze for later use.

Makes ½ cup.

Ancho Chile Butter

> 2 large dried ancho chiles (or
> use New Mexico, pasilla, or
> California variety)
> ½ cup butter

1. Put chiles in a bowl and cover with boiling water. When they are rehydrated, drain them and put them in a food processor or blender; process until finely chopped.

2. In a small saucepan over medium-high heat, melt butter. With machine running, add hot butter to chiles in a fine stream. Blend until color is homogeneous and mixture is smooth.

3. Let stand at room temperature until butter reaches a spoonable consistency. Use immediately, or refrigerate or freeze for later use.

Makes ½ cup.

Savory Rice and Lentil Pilaf is a vegetarian main dish that non-vegetarians might serve as a side dish with steak or another meat. Well spiced, it includes plenty of fresh vegetables, with raisins adding a touch of sweetness.

Broiled chicken breasts, quick and easy, take on a new character when paired with a seasoned butter (see pages 74–75 and this page). Here, butter combined with sun-dried tomatoes tops the poultry.

Blue Cheese Butter

    4 *ounces blue, Stilton, or*
       Roquefort cheese
  ½ *cup unsalted butter*

1. Crumble cheese and place in a food processor or blender.

2. In a small saucepan over medium-high heat, melt butter. With machine running, add hot butter to cheese in a fine stream. Blend until color is homogeneous and mixture is smooth.

3. Let stand at room temperature until butter reaches a spoonable consistency. Use immediately, or refrigerate or freeze for later use.

Makes ½ cup.

Olive-Walnut Butter

  ½ *cup walnut pieces*
  ½ *cup chopped black olives*
  ½ *cup butter*

1. In a food processor or blender, process walnut pieces until they are finely chopped. Add olives.

2. In a small saucepan over medium-high heat, melt butter. With machine running, add hot butter to walnuts and olives in a fine stream. Blend until color is homogeneous and mixture is smooth.

3. Let stand at room temperature until butter reaches a spoonable consistency. Use immediately, or refrigerate or freeze for later use.

Makes ½ cup.

Green Onion and Cilantro Butter

This butter should not be frozen, unless you omit the green onion.

    3 *medium green onions, chopped*
    8 *to 10 sprigs cilantro*
    2 *tablespoons chopped parsley*
  ½ *cup butter*
  ⅛ *teaspoon hot-pepper sauce*

1. In a food processor or blender, process onion, cilantro, and parsley until finely chopped.

2. In a small saucepan over medium-high heat, melt butter. With machine running, add hot butter to onion mixture in a fine stream. Add hot-pepper sauce and blend until color is homogeneous and mixture is smooth.

3. Let stand at room temperature until butter reaches a spoonable consistency. Use immediately, or refrigerate for later use.

Makes ½ cup.

MAKE-AHEAD MAIN DISHES

With a freezer you can cook double batches of a favorite dish and package the second batch for future meals. The recipes that follow are perfect make-ahead-and-freeze main dishes.

Pasta dishes are very popular, and no wonder. They're among the most versatile around. To save time on busy days, make pasta sauces ahead and freeze them. Then all you have to do is cook the pasta and reheat the sauce. One tip: The sauce should be ready to use the minute the pasta is drained. Pasta cools rapidly, and as it cools it begins to stick together. Ideally the pasta should be drained, sauced, served, and eaten within moments of the time it leaves the pot.

For casseroles you plan to reheat in an oven, a handy trick is to line the baking dish with heavy-duty aluminum foil, fill it, freeze until firm, and then remove the dish, folding the foil tightly around the food for storage. This frees your baking dishes for other uses and makes for easy cleanup too. (Do not use foil in the microwave oven.)

Avoid freezing fried foods, because the crisp coating becomes soggy. Crunchy casserole toppings, such as cracker or bread crumbs, will also turn soggy in the freezer, so add them when reheating. Other ingredients to avoid in frozen main dishes are uncooked potatoes, which become mushy and may darken, and hard-cooked egg whites, which toughen.

A microwave oven is ideal for both defrosting and reheating main dishes. Foods that will be defrosted and heated in the microwave should be frozen in ceramic, glass, or microwave-safe plastic containers. Match the size of container to the amount of food you want to freeze.

MEXICAN SHREDDED SPICED BEEF
Carnitas

Use this tasty spiced beef to fill tacos, enchiladas, and burritos. It's a particularly good recipe for the microwave oven, which cuts cooking time by half, saving both energy and time. The recipe makes enough to freeze half for a future meal.

> About 5½ pounds beef chuck roast
> ¼ cup bottled hot chile salsa
> 5 cloves garlic, minced
> 2½ tablespoons chili powder
> 2 tablespoons chopped fresh oregano or 1¾ teaspoons dried
> 1½ teaspoons ground cumin
> 1 can (16 oz) stewed tomatoes
> Salt to taste

1. Preheat oven to 300° F. Trim excess fat from roast.

2. Mix together salsa, garlic, chili powder, oregano, and cumin to make a paste. Spread on roast.

3. Wrap roast in a large piece of aluminum foil, folding edges to seal tightly. Place in roasting pan, with seam of aluminum foil up.

4. Bake until meat is so tender that it will shred easily, 4 to 4½ hours.

5. Unwrap meat; discard fat and bones. Skim fat from drippings and reserve drippings. When roast is cool enough to handle, shred meat.

6. Transfer meat and drippings to a large pan. Stir in tomatoes and their juice, breaking them up into small bits. Heat through. Season with salt; adjust flavors to taste, adding more salsa and seasonings if desired.

Makes about 7 cups shredded beef (enough for about twenty 8-inch tortillas).

Preparation Time About 5 hours, including baking

Timesaver Tip Beef can be made up to 3 days ahead and stored, covered, in refrigerator. It can also be frozen at 0° F up to 3 months. To freeze, package beef in meal-sized servings.

Microwave Version

1. Trim excess fat from roast. Mix together salsa, garlic, chili powder, oregano, and cumin to make a paste. Spread on roast.

2. Place roast in a large (14- by 20-inch) oven cooking bag; squeeze out most of the air and tie securely. Place roast in a large baking dish.

3. Microwave roast on 100% power for 10 minutes. Reduce power to 50% and microwave until meat is so tender it will shred easily, about 2 hours.

4. Unwrap meat; discard fat and bones. Skim fat from drippings and reserve drippings. When roast is cool enough to handle, shred meat.

5. Transfer meat and drippings into a 2-quart casserole. Stir in tomatoes, breaking them into small pieces. Microwave on 70% power until mixture is heated through, about 3 minutes. Season with salt; adjust flavors to taste, adding more salsa and seasonings if desired. Preparation time: about 2½ hours.

ELIOPULOS STEW

You can use the food processor to slice the onions, and also to combine the tomatoes, wine, tomato paste, and brown sugar.

- 2 tablespoons oil
- 3 large onions, thinly sliced
- 1 can (16 oz) tomatoes with their liquid
- 1 cup dry red wine
- 1 can (6 oz) tomato paste
- 2 to 3 teaspoons brown sugar
- ¼ cup dried currants
- 2 bay leaves
- ¾ teaspoon each ground cinnamon and ground cumin, or to taste
  Pinch ground cloves
- 4 to 4¼ pounds lean beef, cut into 1-inch cubes
  Salt and freshly ground pepper to taste
- ½ pound Muenster or jack cheese, cut into ½-inch cubes
- 1 cup broken walnut pieces, toasted

1. In a large, flameproof casserole over medium heat, heat oil. Sauté onions in oil over medium heat until soft, about 5 minutes.

2. Break up tomatoes into small pieces. Stir together tomatoes and their juice, wine, tomato paste, brown sugar, currants, bay leaves, cinnamon, cumin, and cloves; add to casserole.

3. Add beef and simmer, covered, about 2 hours, or until meat is fork-tender. Season to taste with salt and pepper, and adjust other seasonings to taste. If stew is too liquid, uncover pan the last 30 minutes of cooking so that excess liquid will evaporate.

4. *To serve immediately:* Preheat oven to 350° F. Remove casserole from heat and scatter cheese and nuts over top. Bake at 350° F until cheese melts (about 5 minutes).

Serves 6 to 8.

Preparation Time About 2½ hours

Timesaver Tip Stew can be made up to 2 days ahead. Cool to room temperature, cover, and refrigerate or freeze. If you plan to defrost and reheat it in microwave oven, prepare stew in microwave-safe casserole or individual serving dishes. Wrap in heavy-duty foil; seal with freezer tape. Label; freeze at 0° F up to 3 months. To serve, remove foil and cover loosely with waxed paper. Microwave 15 to 20 minutes on Defrost setting. Reheat on 50% power until hot, 3 to 5 minutes. If you plan to defrost and reheat stew in the oven, prepare recipe in an ovenproof casserole or individual heat-and-serve dishes. (See casserole wrapping techniques, page 77.) Wrap in heavy-duty foil; seal with freezer tape. Label; freeze up to 3 months. Remove tape, but not foil. Place dish in cold oven. Turn oven to 375° F and heat 30 to 60 minutes, until mixture is hot.

VEAL RAGOUT

This dish is good with a light red wine such as Gamay Beaujolais. You can use the food processor to chop the onion and tomatoes and to mince the garlic.

- ¼ cup vegetable oil
- 1½ to 1¾ pounds boneless veal shoulder or rump, cut into approximately 2-inch chunks
- 3 tablespoons flour
  Salt
  Freshly ground black pepper
- 1 medium carrot, diced
- 1 stalk celery, diced
- 1 medium onion, chopped
- 1 cup homemade chicken stock or 1 can (10½ oz) chicken broth, preferably low-sodium
- 1 pound small new potatoes, quartered
- ¾ pound tomatoes (2 medium), peeled, seeded, and chopped
- 2 cloves garlic, minced
- 1 bay leaf
- 1 teaspoon finely chopped fresh thyme or ¼ to ½ teaspoon dried, crushed
- ½ pound pearl onions, peeled or ½ pound small boiling onions, peeled and quartered
- ¼ pound mushrooms, quartered
- 2 tablespoons finely chopped parsley, for garnish
- 1½ teaspoons finely grated lemon rind, for garnish

1. In a heavy-bottomed pan over medium heat, heat about 1½ tablespoons of the oil.

2. Pat veal chunks dry with paper towels. Season flour with salt and pepper; toss veal with flour to coat. Brown veal in oil in three batches, adding more oil as necessary. Remove from pan.

3. Add carrots, celery, and onion. Cook over medium-high heat, stirring constantly, until vegetables are lightly browned.

4. Return meat to pan with stock, potatoes, tomatoes, garlic, bay leaf, and thyme.

5. Cover and simmer until veal is tender, 1 to 1½ hours. During the last 30 minutes of cooking, add onions. During the last 10 minutes of cooking, add mushrooms. Season to taste with salt and pepper.

6. Just before serving, combine parsley and lemon rind and sprinkle on top.

Serves 5 to 6.

Preparation Time 2 hours, including simmering

Timesaver Tip Ragout can be frozen up to 4 months.

A make-ahead main dish, Veal Ragout combines a cornucopia of fresh vegetables with chunks of veal. Once cooked, it can be frozen for up to four months.

Pasta sauces are ideal make-ahead-and-freeze main dishes. Here, a classic Italian Sausage and Tomato Sauce served with ziti.

3. Remove pan from heat. Stir in cheese. Use immediately or cool to room temperature and refrigerate or freeze (see Timesaver Tip).

4. *To serve:* Cook 1¼ to 1⅓ pounds fresh or fresh-frozen spinach fettucine, or 8 ounces dried, following package directions. Drain. Toss sauce with pasta.

Makes 2 cups (4 main dish or 6 appetizer servings).

Preparation Time About 15 minutes for sauce

Timesaver Tip Sauce can be made up to 6 hours ahead, covered, and refrigerated, or it can be frozen. To freeze, spoon into a freezer container, cover, label, and freeze at 0° F up to 1 month. To serve, defrost sauce 15 to 20 minutes in microwave oven on Defrost setting, stirring several times, or thaw in refrigerator 8 to 24 hours. Gently warm sauce in a saucepan or microwave oven on 50% power until warmed through, 3 to 5 minutes, whisking frequently and vigorously to bring sauce to a creamy consistency.

SMOKED-SALMON CREAM SAUCE

Try this sauce with spinach fettucine; see step 4 for instructions on cooking the pasta.

   4 *ounces cream cheese*
   1 *cup milk*
   ¼ *pound sliced smoked salmon, cut into approximately ¼-inch pieces*
   ½ *cup cooked fresh or frozen tiny peas, thawed but not cooked*
   1 *large or 2 slender green onions, including green tops, finely sliced*
   1 *to 2 teaspoons lemon juice*
   1 *teaspoon finely chopped fresh dill or ¼ teaspoon dried, or to taste*
   ⅓ *cup freshly grated Parmesan cheese*

1. In a medium saucepan combine cream cheese and milk. Heat, stirring, until mixture is smooth.

2. Stir in smoked salmon, peas, onion, lemon juice, and dill. Cook to heat through.

CREAMY HERB PASTA SAUCE

This sauce is good with fettucine; see step 3 for instructions on cooking the pasta.

   2 *cups half-and-half*
   ½ *cup butter or margarine, cut into 8 chunks*
   ⅔ *cup freshly grated Parmesan, Asiago, or Romano cheese*
   ⅔ *to ¾ cup chopped fresh herbs: any combination of parsley, chives, basil, mint, and oregano*
      Salt and freshly ground pepper to taste

1. Combine half-and-half and butter in a saucepan. Boil gently about 20 minutes, until mixture has reduced to 1½ to 1⅔ cups.

2. Remove pan from heat; whisk in cheese and herbs. Use immediately or cool to room temperature and refrigerate or freeze (see Timesaver Tip).

3. *To serve:* Cook 1¼ to 1⅓ pounds fresh or fresh-frozen fettucine, or 12 ounces dried, following package directions. Drain. Toss with sauce.

Makes 2 cups (4 main dish or 6 appetizer servings).

Preparation Time About 25 minutes for sauce

Timesaver Tip Sauce can be made up to 6 hours ahead, covered and refrigerated, or it can be frozen. To freeze, spoon into a freezer container, cover, label, and freeze at 0° F up to 2 months. To serve, defrost sauce 15 to 20 minutes in microwave oven on Defrost setting, stirring several times, or thaw in refrigerator 8 to 24 hours. Gently warm sauce in a saucepan or microwave oven on 50% power until warmed through, about 3 minutes, whisking frequently and vigorously to bring it to a creamy consistency.

EGGPLANT-MUSHROOM SAUCE

This sauce actually tastes best when made ahead. Serve it with spaghetti; see step 5 for instructions on cooking the pasta.

  1½ tablespoons olive oil
  1 large onion, chopped
  3 cloves garlic, minced
  1 can (28 oz) tomatoes, undrained
  ¼ cup dry red or white wine or vermouth
  1 eggplant (1 to 1½ lbs), unpeeled and cut in ¾-inch cubes
  2 cups sliced mushrooms (¼ lb)
  2 teaspoons each *finely chopped fresh basil and oregano* or ¾ teaspoon each dried
  ½ teaspoon sugar
     Salt and freshly ground pepper to taste

1. In a wide-bottomed pan or skillet with high sides over medium-high heat, heat oil. Add onion and garlic; sauté about 2 minutes.

2. Break tomatoes into bits. Add to pan with their juice, wine, eggplant, mushrooms, herbs, and sugar.

3. Cover pan and simmer 5 minutes. Remove cover and cook over medium heat until sauce reduces and thickens, 10 to 15 minutes.

4. Season to taste with salt and pepper. Cool to room temperature and refrigerate or freeze (see Timesaver Tip).

5. *To serve:* Cook 12 ounces dried spaghetti, following package directions. Drain. Serve sauce over pasta. Serve with a generous amount of freshly grated Parmesan cheese.

Make 5 to 6 cups (5 to 6 servings).

Preparation Time 30 to 35 minutes for sauce

Timesaver Tip Sauce can be made up to 2 days ahead, covered, and refrigerated, or it can be frozen. To freeze, spoon into freezer container, cover, label, and freeze at 0° F up to 4 months. To serve, defrost sauce 20 to 30 minutes in microwave oven on Defrost setting, stirring several times, or thaw in refrigerator 8 to 24 hours. Gently warm sauce in saucepan or in microwave oven on 50% power, 3 to 5 minutes, stirring several times.

ITALIAN SAUSAGE AND TOMATO SAUCE

This sauce is good with ziti or rigatoni; see step 5 for instructions on cooking the pasta. You can use the food processor to mince the garlic, slice the onion, and chop the herbs.

  1 to 1¼ pounds mild or hot fresh Italian sausage, or a combination, cut into ¾-inch pieces
  1 large onion, thinly sliced
  3 large cloves garlic, minced
  1¼ to 1½ pounds fresh tomatoes, peeled and coarsely chopped, or 1 can (28 oz) whole peeled tomatoes, drained and coarsely chopped
  ¼ to ⅓ cup Marsala wine
  ¼ cup fresh basil leaves or 3 tablespoons chopped parsley plus 2 teaspoons dried basil
     Salt and freshly ground pepper to taste

1. In a wide-bottomed pan or skillet with high sides over medium heat, brown sausage for about 5 minutes.

2. Push sausage to side of pan. Add onions and garlic; sauté in sausage fat about 2 minutes. Pour off all but a thin film of fat.

3. Add tomatoes and Marsala to pan. If using dried basil, add it now. Cook over medium heat until sauce reduces and thickens, about 5 to 10 minutes.

4. Stir in fresh basil or parsley. Season to taste with salt and pepper, if necessary. Use immediately or cool to room temperature and refrigerate or freeze (see Timesaver Tip).

5. *To serve:* Cook 8 ounces ziti or rigatoni, following package directions. Drain. Serve sauce over pasta. Top each serving with a spoonful of ricotta cheese.

Makes 4 cups (4 to 5 servings).

Preparation Time About 20 minutes for sauce

Timesaver Tip Sauce can be made up to 2 days ahead, covered and refrigerated, or it can be frozen. To freeze, spoon into a freezer container, cover, label, and freeze at 0° F up to 1 month. To serve, defrost sauce 15 to 20 minutes in microwave oven on Defrost setting, or thaw in refrigerator 8 to 24 hours. Gently warm sauce in saucepan or in a microwave oven on 50% power until heated through, 3 to 5 minutes. Stir sauce several times during microwave defrosting.

CHEDDAR AND CHILE SAUCE

Here's a new twist to an old standby, macaroni and cheese. Try this sauce with spinach or artichoke pasta, instead of elbow macaroni (see step 3 for directions on cooking the pasta).

    ¼   cup butter or margarine
    ¼   cup flour
    3   cups milk
    1   teaspoon salt
    ½   teaspoon hot-pepper sauce
    ½   teaspoon ground cumin
        (optional)
    ½   pound sharp Cheddar cheese,
        shredded
    1   jar (4 oz) diced pimiento
    1   can (4 oz) diced green chiles
    1   cup black ripe olive slices

1. In a 2-quart saucepan over medium heat, melt butter. Stir in flour and cook, stirring, until mixture is smooth and bubbly. Remove from heat; whisk in milk. Return to heat and bring to a boil, stirring constantly; mixture will thicken. Boil and stir 1 minute. Stir in salt, hot pepper sauce, and cumin (if used).

2. Remove pan from heat; add cheese, pimiento, green chiles, and olives, stirring until cheese melts. Adjust seasonings to taste.

3. *To serve:* Preheat oven to 350° F. In boiling salted water, cook 1 pound elbow macaroni, following package directions. Drain; toss with sauce. Adjust seasonings if necessary. Pour into a 2-quart casserole; top with an additional ½ pound sharp Cheddar cheese, shredded. Cover; bake until mixture is heated through and cheese is melted, 15 to 20 minutes.

Serves 4 to 6.

Preparation Time About 25 to 30 minutes for sauce

Timesaver Tip Sauce can be made up to 6 hours ahead, covered, and refrigerated, or it can be frozen. To freeze, spoon into a freezer container, cover, label, and freeze at 0° F up to 2 months. To serve, defrost sauce 15 to 20 minutes in microwave oven on Defrost setting, stirring several times, or thaw in refrigerator 8 to 24 hours. Gently warm sauce in a saucepan or microwave oven on 50% power until warmed through, about 3 minutes, whisking frequently and vigorously to bring it to a creamy consistency.

TOMATO AND PANCETTA SAUCE

You'll enjoy the convenience of preparing this sauce in the oven. Serve it with fusilli (see step 5). You can use the food processor to chop both the fresh and the sun-dried tomatoes.

    3   pounds (approximately 6 me-
        dium) tomatoes, peeled, seed-
        ed, and coarsely chopped
    3   tablespoons finely chopped
        sun-dried tomatoes packed
        in oil
    2   tablespoons oil from
        sun-dried tomatoes
    1   tablespoon olive oil
    ½   pound pancetta or slab
        bacon, diced
    ¼   cup finely chopped parsley
        Salt, if necessary

1. Preheat oven to 350° F. Combine fresh tomatoes with sun-dried tomatoes; set aside.

2. Pour oils into a 9- by 13-inch baking dish; place in the oven to heat the oil, about 2 to 3 minutes. Add pancetta and return to the oven until pancetta starts to brown, tossing occasionally with a spatula, about 5 minutes. Stir in tomatoes.

3. Bake 30 to 35 minutes, stirring occasionally, until tomatoes are cooked and form a sauce.

4. Remove from oven; stir in parsley. Season with salt, if necessary.

5. *To serve:* Cook 1 pound dried pasta, such as fusilli (spiral-shaped) in salted water, following package directions. Drain. Serve sauce over pasta and pass ⅓ cup freshly grated Parmesan cheese at table.

Makes 4 main-dish or 6 appetizer servings.

Preparation Time 45 to 50 minutes for sauce

Timesaver Tip Sauce can be made up to 6 hours ahead, covered, and refrigerated, or it can be frozen. To freeze, spoon into a freezer container, cover, label, and freeze at 0° F up to 2 months. To serve, defrost sauce 15 to 20 minutes in microwave oven on Defrost setting, stirring several times, or thaw in refrigerator 8 to 24 hours. Gently warm sauce in a saucepan or microwave oven on 50% power until warmed through, about 3 minutes, whisking frequently and vigorously to bring it to a creamy consistency.

SALSA VERDE WITH TUNA

This sauce is good with a thin pasta such as thin spaghetti; see step 3 for instructions on cooking the pasta.

    1   cup packed parsley sprigs
    1½   cups packed basil leaves
         (see Note)
    2   large cloves garlic
    1   can (2 oz) flat anchovy
         fillets, drained
    ¼   cup olive oil
    1   to 2 teaspoons lemon juice
    1   can (6½ oz) water-packed
         tuna, drained
         Freshly ground pepper to taste

1. In a food processor or blender, process parsley, basil, garlic, anchovies, oil, and lemon juice to a purée.

2. By hand, stir in tuna. Season to taste with pepper. Use immediately or cool to room temperature and refrigerate or freeze (see Timesaver Tip).

3. *To serve:* Cook 8 ounces thin tubular pasta, such as thin spaghetti, following package directions. Drain. Toss pasta with 2 tablespoons olive oil, then with sauce. Top with sliced black olives, slivered dried tomatoes in oil *(pumate)*, or freshly grated Parmesan cheese.

Makes 1¼ cups (3 to 4 servings).

Preparation Time About 10 minutes for sauce

Timesaver Tip Sauce can be made up to 1 day ahead, covered and refrigerated, or it can be frozen. To freeze, spoon into a freezer container, cover, label, and freeze at 0° F up to 3 months. To serve, defrost sauce 8 to 12 minutes in microwave oven on Defrost setting, stirring several times, or thaw in refrigerator 8 to 24 hours. Gently warm sauce in saucepan or in microwave oven on 50% power, 1 to 3 minutes. Sauce should be at room temperature or barely warm when tossed with pasta.

Note When basil is unavailable, use 2½ cups packed parsley sprigs and 1½ to 2 tablespoons dried basil.

CHÈVRE AND WALNUT SAUCE

Serve this sauce with fettucine; see step 4 for instructions on cooking the pasta.

    2 cups half-and-half
    8 ounces plain chèvre or
       10 ounces coated (remove
       coating)
    2 cloves garlic, minced
    ¾ cups coarsely chopped
       toasted walnuts
    ⅓ cup finely chopped parsley
       Salt and freshly ground
       pepper to taste

1. In a medium saucepan combine half-and-half, chèvre, and garlic. Heat, stirring until mixture is creamy and smooth. Bring to a boil.

2. Boil gently about 10 minutes to thicken sauce and reduce it to about 2¼ cups. Stir occasionally at first, then frequently the last few minutes to prevent scorching.

3. Remove from heat; stir in walnuts and parsley. Season to taste with salt and pepper. Use immediately or cool to room temperature and refrigerate or freeze (see Timesaver Tip).

4. *To serve:* Cook 1¼ to 1⅓ pounds fresh or frozen fettucine, or 12 ounces dried, following package directions. Drain. Toss with sauce.

Makes 2¼ cups (4 main-dish or 6 appetizer servings).

Preparation Time 20 to 25 minutes for sauce

Timesaver Tip Sauce can be made up to 6 hours ahead, covered and refrigerated, or it can be frozen. To freeze, spoon into a freezer container, cover, label, and freeze at 0° F up to 1 month. To serve, defrost sauce 12 to 18 minutes in microwave oven on Defrost setting, stirring several times, or thaw in refrigerator 8 to 24 hours. Gently warm sauce in a saucepan, or in a microwave oven on 50% power until warmed through, 3 to 5 minutes, whisking vigorously and frequently to bring sauce to a creamy consistency.

For a light, elegant approach to pasta, try Smoked-Salmon Cream Sauce (see page 80) with fettucine. Cream cheese makes it rich, while peas and green onions add color.

DINNER FOR A WINTER NIGHT

Make-Ahead Cheese and Chile Soufflé

Orange and Watercress Salad

Rolls and Butter

Milk or Beer

Fresh Fruit Sorbet in Seconds (see page 123)

When it's cold outside, something hot and spicy is always welcome. Chile salsa adds its warmth to a make-ahead soufflé: After mixing it up, you can refrigerate it up to 24 hours, or freeze it and then bake it direct from the freezer. Serve it with a crisp watercress salad, and finish the meal with the tang of fresh fruit sorbet.

MAKE-AHEAD CHEESE AND CHILE SOUFFLÉ

This dish can be partially completed, refrigerated up to 24 hours, and then finished, or the soufflé mixture can be made ahead and frozen, then baked direct from the freezer. Although the soufflé won't rise as high as usual when it has been frozen, the resulting dish is nonetheless surprisingly light and delicious.

    ¼ cup butter or margarine
    ¼ cup flour
    1 cup milk
    1½ cups (6 oz) shredded
       Cheddar cheese
    2 to 4 tablespoons bottled hot
       chile salsa, or to taste
    ½ teaspoon salt
    6 eggs, separated

1. Preheat oven to 375° F. Lightly butter an 8-cup soufflé dish; set aside.

2. In a medium saucepan over medium heat, melt butter. Whisk in flour until mixture is smooth. Whisk in milk.

3. Whisk sauce over medium-high heat until it boils and thickens. Remove pan from heat.

4. Add cheese, salsa, and salt; stir until cheese melts. Beat in egg yolks.

5. In large bowl of electric mixer, beat egg whites until they hold soft, moist peaks. Stir one fourth of whites into cheese mixture to lighten it; fold in remaining whites.

6. Pour mixture into prepared soufflé dish and bake in preheated oven 30 to 40 minutes.

Serves 4 to 6.

Preparation Time 20 minutes plus baking time

Timesaver Tip *To make ahead:* Prepare recipe through step 4. Cover surface of mixture with wax paper and refrigerate up to 24 hours. Put egg whites in a bowl, cover, and refrigerate. To complete dish, bring cheese mixture and egg whites to room temperature (this can be done quickly in a microwave oven at a low setting) and continue with steps 5 and 6. (Refrigeration is not necessary if recipe is prepared only a few hours in advance.)

To make ahead and freeze: Prepare recipe through step 5. Wrap freezer-to-oven soufflé dish in aluminum foil. Label, date, and freeze up to 2 months. To serve, preheat oven to 375° F. Remove foil and put soufflé dish directly into oven from freezer; do not thaw. Bake 50 to 55 minutes. Soufflé will be puffy and the top well browned. Serve immediately.

ORANGE AND WATERCRESS SALAD

    1 bunch watercress
       Half a red onion, cut in
       thin rings
       Basic, Mild, or Grapefruit
       Vinaigrette (see page 99)
    1 orange, peeled and separated
       into segments

1. Wash and pick over watercress; tear into bite-sized pieces.

2. Combine watercress and onion rings with the vinaigrette of your choice, and toss until watercress and onion rings are well coated.

3. Divide watercress-onion mixture among 4 to 6 salad plates. Top each serving with some of the orange segments.

Serves 4 to 6.

Preparation Time About 15 minutes

No-fuss dinner: Make-Ahead Cheese and Chile Soufflé, Orange and Watercress Salad, and Papaya Sorbet (see page 123), ready in minutes.

A wealth of produce invites the cook to prepare simple, quick dishes—like the ones in this chapter—that capitalize on fresh flavor.

Vegetables, Salads & Side Dishes

The incomparable flavor of fresh vegetables—in salads or on their own—would be worth almost any culinary effort. But in fact they're at their best when prepared simply, which means they're a significant part of the repertoire of the timesaver cook. In this chapter you will find light salads, microwaved and sautéed vegetables, and pasta and rice side dishes to round out the dinner menu, as well as hearty salads that are a meal in themselves. There's also a selection of seasoned butters (page 96) that make simple, savory toppings for vegetables, and a quartet of vinaigrettes (page 99) for dressing salads.

FRESH FROM THE GREENGROCER

Fresh fruits and vegetables are not just a way to a balanced diet; they are an integral part of today's lighter cuisine. And, happily, with the high-quality produce that is available in most markets today, simple preparation is best. That makes fresh vegetables an important component of timesaver cooking.

For best results choose vegetables that are in peak season—their quality and price are best. Signs of freshness include crispness, firmness, and bright, natural colors. Avoid vegetables that look wilted, withered, or leathery, and those that have any signs of decay or bruises.

Vegetables can be cooked by a variety of methods. Most of the vegetables in this chapter are cooked by boiling, steaming, sautéing or stir-frying, or microwaving. Generally, vegetables taste best and retain the most nutrients when cooked only until crisp-tender—when they can just be pierced by a fork and still remain firm.

Simple preparation points up the fresh taste, texture, and color of vegetables. Highly seasoned toppings and fancy sauces only mask a vegetable's natural flavor and color—and they are time-consuming to make. A knob of butter or seasoned butter (see page 96) or a sprinkling of fresh herbs is all the embellishment they really need.

TIMESAVING, NUTRITIOUS WAYS TO COOK VEGETABLES

Boiling

The best way to boil vegetables is in just enough water to prevent scorching. Cover the pan with a tight-fitting lid so that steam won't escape. Cook vegetables until crisp-tender. Any leftover cooking liquid can be frozen for use later in soups.

Steaming

Steaming is cooking vegetables in a perforated container over simmering water. Any vegetable that can be boiled can be steamed. Steamed vegetables retain more of their vitamins than do boiled ones; however, steaming takes longer. To shorten steaming time, cut vegetables into small, thin pieces. To steam, place vegetables in a steaming rack or in the top of a steamer pan, place over simmering water, cover pan, and cook until vegetables are crisp-tender.

Sautéing

Sautéing is quick-cooking in a small amount of fat. This method retains bright colors, crisp textures, and nutrients. The technique of stir-frying is essentially the same.

Microwaving

Microwave ovens are excellent for cooking vegetables. The vegetables come out crisp-tender, with their natural colors still vibrant. And nutrition research indicates that many vegetables lose fewer water-soluble nutrients such as vitamin C when microwaved, due to the shorter cooking time and lower amount of water needed. The shorter cooking time also means that the fresh flavor is retained.

MICROWAVING FRESH VEGETABLES

1. Refer to the chart on page 91 to determine the approximate cooking and standing time for a given amount of a vegetable. Weights listed are for fresh vegetables as purchased, before trimming, peeling, and other preparation.

2. Cut vegetables into uniform pieces for even cooking. To speed cooking, shred or thinly slice vegetables, and peel the coarse outer layer from asparagus (unless it's pencil-thin) and broccoli stems. Place in a round microwave-safe baking or serving dish. Put the woody stems of asparagus and broccoli, or thicker portions if vegetables are not of uniform size, toward the outside of the dish. Vegetables to be cooked whole and unpeeled, such as potatoes and winter squash, need to be pierced with a fork to allow steam to escape. Left unpierced, the vegetable might explode. Arrange potatoes 1 inch apart in a star pattern on a paper towel, thicker ends toward the outside. See the facing page for special instructions for cooking artichokes and corn on the cob.

3. Cook most vegetables with a few tablespoons of water to provide steam. Steam contributes both speed and even cooking. Cover the dish with a lid or plastic wrap.

4. Microwave on 100% power according to the time recommended on the chart. Halfway through cooking, stir vegetables, rearrange, or turn them over.

5. Let vegetables stand, covered, according to the time recommended in the chart. Standing time is very short or unneccessary for some vegetables, but for large, dense vegetables like winter squash, or a whole head of cauliflower, it allows for thorough cooking without overdoing the outer edge.

6. Remember that cooking and standing times are approximate and will vary with the maturity, shape, size, and starting temperature of vegetables.

7. Season vegetables with salt and pepper after cooking.

MICROWAVING CORN ON THE COB

Fresh corn can be microwaved right in its husk. Strip the husk back from the cob, leaving it attached at the bottom. Remove the corn silk. Brush the ear with melted butter or margarine, and pull the husks back over the corn. Run corn quickly under cold water to add moisture for cooking. Place ears in a spoke pattern on paper towel in microwave oven. Microwave as directed in the chart on page 91, rearranging and turning ears once.

To microwave husked corn, remove husks and corn silks. Rinse corn and brush with melted butter or margarine. Roll each ear in a square of waxed paper, twisting ends to seal. Microwave as directed above.

MICROWAVING FRESH ARTICHOKES

Cut off the stem and about an inch of the pointed top of each artichoke. With scissors, snip off the prickly tips of each leaf. Rinse. Rub the cut edges of leaves with lemon juice to prevent browning. Wrap each artichoke in a square of waxed paper, twisting ends to seal. Microwave as directed in the chart on page 91, turning artichokes once.

To serve hot, accompany artichoke with melted butter or margarine, or one of the seasoned butters on page 96, melted, or with Hollandaise sauce. To serve cold, refrigerate artichoke until chilled. Open artichoke like a flower to reach interior, pull out tender center cone of leaves, and scrape out the fuzzy choke with a spoon. Serve with vinaigrette or mayonnaise, in cavity, if desired. The artichoke cavity can also be filled with a salad mixture, such as shrimp or tuna.

Vegetables cooked in the microwave retain both color and nutritive value. Here, a mix of zucchini, summer squash, eggplant, and peeled, seeded tomatoes is accompanied by Mustard Butter and Dill Butter (see page 96).

The microwave oven is ideal for cooking vegetables, including corn on the cob and artichokes (see page 89).

MICROWAVING FRESH VEGETABLES

Cooking time is given in minutes and assumes the vegetable is covered and the microwave is operating on 100% power. Standing time is given in minutes.

Vegetable	Amount	Approximate Cooking Time	Standing Time
Artichokes (See instructions, page 89)	1 (6 to 8 oz)	5 to 8	5
	2	8 to 10	5
	4	12 to 14	5
Asparagus (Pare stalks except on very thin spears)	1 lb plus 2 tbsp water	4 to 7	1
Beans, green or wax Cut into 1½-in pieces	1 lb plus 2 tbsp water	5 to 7	2
Broccoli Cut into spears (pare stalks)	1 lb plus 2 tbsp water	6 to 8	2
Brussels sprouts	1 tub (10 oz) plus 1 tbsp water	5 to 7	2
	1 lb plus 2 tbsp water	8 to 10	3
Cabbage Chopped or shredded	4 cups (about 1 lb) plus 2 tbsp water	6 to 8	0
Wedges	4 (about 1 lb) plus 2 tbsp water	5 to 7	2
Carrots Sliced into rounds	1 lb plus 2 tbsp water	6 to 8	1
Cauliflower Cut into flowerets	1 lb plus 2 tbsp water	6 to 8	2
Whole	1 to 1½ lbs plus 2 tbsp water	11 to 13	3
Corn on the cob (See instructions, page 89)	1 ear	2 to 3	3
	2 ears	3 to 4	3
	4 ears	8½ to 10	3
Eggplant Cubed	1 lb plus 2 tbsp water	6 to 8	1
Whole (pierce skin)	1 to 1¼ lbs	4 to 7	3
Onions Small, whole	1 lb plus 2 tbsp water	4 to 8	2
Parsnips Sliced	1 lb plus 2 tbsp water	6 to 8	2
Peas, green	1½ lbs plus 3 tbsp water	5 to 7	1
Peas, snow (pea pods)	1 lb plus 2 tbsp water	4 to 6	1
Potatoes, new Small, whole (pierce skin)	1 lb (6 to 8) plus 3 tbsp water	8 to 12	3
Potatoes, white or sweet Whole for baking (pierce skin)	1 (6 to 8 oz)	4 to 6	5
	2	6 to 8	5
	4	8 to 12	5
	(Touch potatoes at end of cooking time. If they are *very* hard, cook another minute or two, then let them stand. They will finish cooking in the standing time.)		
Spinach Washed, whole	1 lb (water that clings to leaves is enough moisture)	4 to 6	0
Squash, spaghetti Whole (pierce skin)	1 (4 to 5 lbs)	15 to 20	5
Squash, summer	1 lb plus 2 tbsp water	4 to 6	0
Squash, winter Whole (pierce skin)	1 (1 lb)	6 to 8	5
	2 (¾ lb each)	7 to 9	5
Zucchini Sliced ½ in thick	1 lb plus 2 tbsp water	4 to 6	0

TIMESAVER TIP

When you're entertaining, you want to have as much done ahead of time as possible. One help is to serve a vegetable purée (at right), which can be made ahead and reheated without the risk of losing color or texture. Another way is to microwave vegetables in two steps. First cook the vegetable until it is just starting to get tender (refer to the chart on page 91), then rinse under cold running water to stop the cooking. Cover and refrigerate. Just before serving, melt butter or margarine (or one of the seasoned butters on page 96) in a glass baking dish or microwave-safe serving dish in the microwave on 100% power, about 30 seconds. Add vegetables; toss to coat with butter, and microwave until crisp-tender and heated through, stirring once.

VEGETABLE PURÉES

A nice variation for serving vegetables, purées are good with broiled, baked, or sautéed meats. Almost any vegetable is suitable; the list below gives some suggestions. If you wish to serve more than one, prepare them separately and serve them side by side or swirled together on the plate. Purées can also be made into soup (see instructions at right).

> 1 pound fresh vegetables, trimmed
> 1 tablespoon butter or margarine
> ¼ to ½ cup half-and-half
> Salt and freshly ground pepper to taste

1. Cut vegetables into pieces of even size. Steam until tender in a small amount of water or microwave as directed in the chart on page 91. Drain, reserving any liquid for soups, if desired.

2. Place vegetables and butter in food processor or blender. Process until smooth.

3. With machine running, slowly add half-and-half to make a smooth, creamy purée. Season to taste with salt and pepper.

Serves 4 to 6.

Preparation Time About 15 minutes

Timesaver Tip Recipe can be prepared up to a day ahead and reheated in a saucepan over low heat or in a microwave oven.

Variations Herbs and spices add another dimension to vegetable purées. Here are a few suggestions.

Carrots Add dried dill weed to taste.

Cauliflower Add curry powder or ½ cup shredded Swiss or Cheddar cheese. Dust with paprika or serve with a purée of contrasting color.

Broccoli Add a pinch of cayenne pepper.

Parsnips Add ground allspice or ground nutmeg to taste.

Spinach Add ground nutmeg to taste.

Zucchini, pattypan, or crookneck squash Add a few sprigs of dill weed.

Puréed Vegetable Soup Blend vegetable purée with enough chicken or beef stock to make a soupy mixture. Gently heat in saucepan until warmed through.

GRATED ZUCCHINI AND YELLOW SQUASH

A simple sauté that needs no embellishment.

> 1 to 2 teaspoons butter or margarine
> 2 small zucchini and 2 medium yellow squash (¾ pound total), grated
> Salt and freshly ground pepper to taste

In a large skillet over medium heat, melt butter. Add squash and sauté, stirring frequently until tender, 2 to 3 minutes. Season to taste with salt and pepper.

Serves 4 to 5.

Preparation Time 7 to 10 minutes

Variation Sprinkle with 2 to 3 tablespoons freshly grated Parmesan cheese just before serving.

SAUTÉED CHERRY TOMATOES

A quick and tasty summer vegetable dish.

> 1 tablespoon olive oil, butter, or margarine
> 1 pint cherry tomatoes, stemmed
> 2 to 3 tablespoons finely chopped parsley or a mixture of parsley and fresh basil, oregano, or thyme
> Salt and freshly ground pepper to taste

1. In a large skillet over medium heat, heat oil. Add tomatoes and sauté, stirring occasionally, about 2 to 3 minutes. Cook until tomatoes are soft, but do not let them burst.

2. Sprinkle with herbs. Toss to coat.

3. Season to taste with salt and pepper.

Serves 4 to 6.

Preparation Time 7 to 10 minutes

SAVORY WHITE BEANS

This robust bean dish is excellent with lamb.

> 1 tablespoon olive oil
> 1 small clove garlic, minced
> 1 can (14 or 16 oz) white kidney beans (canellini), drained
> 1 to 1½ teaspoons finely chopped fresh oregano, sage, or rosemary or ¼ to ½ teaspoon dried
> 2 tablespoons finely chopped parsley
> ½ cup chopped tomato
> 1 to 2 teaspoons red wine vinegar
> Freshly ground pepper to taste

1. In a small saucepan over medium heat, heat oil and garlic. Cook, stirring, about 1 minute.

2. Add beans and herbs; cook to heat through.

3. Stir in parsley, tomato, and red wine vinegar. Cook about 30 seconds longer. Season with pepper and adjust other seasonings to taste.

Serves 4.

Preparation Time About 15 minutes

Microwave Version

1. In a casserole heat oil and garlic on 100% power 2 minutes.

2. Add beans and herbs; microwave on 100% power about 1 minute.

3. Stir in parsley, tomato, and red wine vinegar. Microwave on 100% power 20 to 30 seconds. Season with pepper and adjust other seasonings to taste. Preparation time same as above.

Sweet cherry tomatoes make a colorful and quick sauté. Buy them at the height of their season, when their flavor is at a peak; this simple treatment of olive oil and herbs is all they need.

93

For speedy cooking, boil tiny new potatoes, then sauce them with a combination of butter, mustard, and chives to make a zesty vegetable dish.

MUSTARD-TOSSED POTATOES

A savory sauce makes a new presentation for tiny boiled potatoes.

   8 to 12 tiny new potatoes
      (1¼ to 1½ pounds)
   3 tablespoons butter, softened
1½ tablespoon Dijon mustard
   2 tablespoons finely chopped
      chives, green-onion tops,
      or parsley

1. Using a paring knife or vegetable peeler, remove a thin layer of skin around the middle of each potato, leaving the skin intact on the top and bottom. Rinse potatoes and put in saucepan with water to cover. Bring to a boil, covered, and boil gently until potatoes are tender, 15 to 20 minutes. Drain.

2. In a small bowl blend butter and mustard and add chives.

3. In pan or serving bowl, toss hot potatoes in butter mixture to coat. Serve immediately.

Serves 4 to 6.

Preparation Time About 30 minutes

BOURBON-MINT CARROTS

A good accompaniment to lamb or pork. You can use the food processor to slice the carrots.

- ¾ pound carrots, thinly sliced or cut into 2-inch-long matchstick pieces
- 2 tablespoons bourbon (see Note)
- 1 tablespoon water
- 1 tablespoon butter or margarine (optional)
- About 2 teaspoons finely chopped fresh mint or ½ to 1 teaspoon dried crumbled mint
- Salt and freshly ground pepper to taste

1. Place carrots, bourbon, water, and butter (if used) in a medium saucepan. Cook over medium-high heat about 5 minutes, or until carrots are crisp-tender.

2. Stir in mint. Season to taste with salt and pepper.

Serves 4 to 5.

Preparation Time About 15 minutes

Note Brandy can be substituted for the bourbon.

TOMATOES PROVENÇALE

These tomatoes, herbed and scented with garlic, are especially good when served with simply prepared fresh fish or shellfish.

- 2 large firm tomatoes
- 1 or 2 small cloves garlic
- ¾ to 1 teaspoon chopped fresh rosemary or basil or ¼ to ½ teaspoon dried
- Salt and freshly ground pepper to taste
- Olive oil

1. Slice tomatoes horizontally into 4 slices, each ½ inch thick.

2. Peel and split garlic; mash slightly with the side of a knife. Rub garlic on cut surfaces of tomatoes.

3. Arrange tomatoes on broiler pan. Sprinkle with herbs, salt, and pepper, and drizzle lightly with oil.

4. Broil until surfaces are blistered. Serve immediately.

Serves 4.

Preparation Time About 15 minutes

Variation Sprinkle tomatoes with ¼ cup freshly grated Parmesan or Romano cheese. Broil until cheese is lightly browned and bubbly.

GARLIC-SAUTÉED SWISS CHARD

Choose chard with white stalks (or, for red swiss chard, red stalks) and dark green leaves. The leaves should be crisp and unblemished; yellow leaves indicate overmaturity. Stems take longer to cook than leaves, so start by cooking them alone, then add the leaves when the stems are crisp-tender.

- About 1 pound red or green Swiss chard
- 1 tablespoon olive oil
- 2 cloves garlic, peeled and cut in half lengthwise
- 1 to 2 teaspoons lemon juice
- Salt and freshly ground pepper to taste

1. Wash and trim chard. Slice stems into ½-inch pieces and roughly chop leaves.

2. In a large skillet over medium heat, heat oil. Sauté garlic in oil several minutes, until it begins to brown. Remove garlic and discard.

3. Add chard stems to skillet. Cover and cook over medium heat until crisp-tender, 3 to 4 minutes.

4. Add chard leaves. Sauté, stirring constantly until leaves are wilted, about 1 minute.

5. Season to taste with lemon juice, salt, and pepper.

Serves 4 to 5.

Preparation Time About 20 minutes

HOT SLAW

This is a good accompaniment to pork dishes, and to cold cuts and sandwiches as well. If you like, you can sprinkle in caraway seeds for an added piquant touch. You can use the food processor to shred the cabbage.

- 1 tablespoon butter or margarine or vegetable oil
- 4 cups shredded red cabbage
- 2 to 3 tablespoons red wine vinegar
- ¾ to 1 teaspoon sugar
- Salt and freshly ground black pepper

1. In a medium saucepan over medium heat, melt butter. Stir in cabbage, 2 tablespoons vinegar, and ¾ teaspoon sugar.

2. Cook uncovered over medium heat, stirring occasionally until cabbage is limp but still crisp, 3 to 5 minutes. Add more vinegar and sugar to taste. Season with salt and pepper.

Serves 4 to 6.

Preparation Time 10 minutes

Microwave Version

1. In a medium casserole, melt butter on 100% power for 30 seconds.

2. Add cabbage, 2 tablespoons vinegar, and ¾ teaspoon sugar and microwave on 100% power 1 to 3 minutes, stirring after 1 minute. Add more vinegar and sugar to taste. Season with salt and pepper.

Preparation Time About 10 minutes

SAUTÉED SNOW PEAS

Snow peas remain succulent and colorful with this quick preparation.

>   1 to 2 teaspoons butter
>   or margarine
>   ½ pound snow peas or sugar
>   snap peas, strings removed
>   Pinch sugar
>   Salt and freshly ground
>   pepper to taste

In a large skillet over medium heat, melt butter. Add peas and sauté, stirring frequently until tender, about 3 to 4 minutes. Season to taste with sugar, salt, and pepper.

Serves 4.

Preparation Time 7 to 10 minutes

BUTTER-STEAMED SPINACH

This simple method of cooking spinach preserves the nutrients, color, and flavor.

>   1 to 2 teaspoons butter
>   or margarine
>   1 pound fresh spinach, washed,
>   stemmed, and torn into
>   small pieces
>   Ground allspice or ground
>   nutmeg (optional)
>   Salt and freshly ground
>   pepper to taste

1. In a large skillet over medium heat, melt butter. Add spinach to skillet; cover and cook over medium heat 2 to 3 minutes.

2. Remove cover and stir spinach until leaves are wilted and tender, about 1 minute. Season with allspice, if used, and salt and pepper to taste.

Serves 4.

Preparation Time 15 minutes

Microwave Version Melt butter in casserole on 100% power for 20 seconds. Add spinach. Cover and microwave on 100% power 1 to 2 minutes, stirring after 1 minute. Preparation time same as above.

SEASONED BUTTERS

Make these seasoned butters ahead and refrigerate or freeze (see timesaver tip), ready to slice onto steaming fresh vegetables, hot pasta, or grilled seafood. Each takes about 10 minutes to prepare.

Lemon-Parsley Butter

>   ½ cup butter, softened
>   3 tablespoons finely chopped
>   parsley
>   1 teaspoon finely grated
>   lemon rind
>   1 tablespoon lemon juice
>   Pinch white pepper

1. In small bowl of electric mixer, in a food processor, or by hand, beat butter until soft and light.

2. Add parsley, lemon rind, lemon juice, and pepper; mix to blend well.

3. Shape into a roll, wrap in plastic wrap, and refrigerate until firm.

Makes ½ cup.

Timesaver Tip Recipe can be refrigerated for up to 2 weeks or frozen up to 4 months. To freeze, wrap again in heavy-duty aluminum foil.

Lime-Cilantro Butter

>   ½ cup butter, softened
>   1 to 2 tablespoons finely
>   chopped cilantro
>   ½ teaspoon finely grated
>   lime rind
>   4 teaspoons lime juice
>   Pinch white pepper

1. In small bowl of electric mixer, in a food processor, or by hand, beat butter until soft and light.

2. Add cilantro, lime rind, lime juice, and pepper; mix to blend well.

3. Shape into a roll, wrap in plastic wrap, and refrigerate until firm.

Makes ½ cup.

Timesaver Tip Recipe can be refrigerated for up to 2 weeks or frozen up to 4 months. To freeze, wrap again in heavy-duty aluminum foil.

Mustard Butter

>   ½ cup butter, softened
>   1½ tablespoons finely chopped
>   parsley
>   2 teaspoons lemon juice
>   2½ tablespoons Dijon mustard

1. In small bowl of electric mixer, in a food processor, or by hand, beat butter until soft and light.

2. Add parsley, lemon juice, and mustard; mix to blend well.

3. Shape into a roll, wrap in plastic wrap, and refrigerate until firm.

Makes ½ cup.

Timesaver Tip Recipe can be refrigerated for up to 2 weeks or frozen up to 4 months. To freeze, wrap again in heavy-duty aluminum foil.

Dill Butter

>   ½ cup butter, softened
>   1 to 2 tablespoons finely
>   chopped fresh dill or
>   1½ teaspoons dried
>   1 teaspoon finely grated
>   lemon rind
>   2 teaspoons lemon juice
>   Pinch white pepper

1. In small bowl of electric mixer, in a food processor, or by hand, beat butter until soft and light.

2. Add dill, lemon rind, lemon juice, and pepper; mix to blend well.

3. Shape into a roll, wrap in plastic wrap, and refrigerate until firm.

Makes ½ cup.

Timesaver Tip Recipe can be refrigerated for up to 2 weeks or frozen up to 4 months. To freeze, wrap again in heavy-duty aluminum foil.

LUNCHEON AND SUPPER SALADS

When it's too hot to cook, or when all you want is a light, fresh meal, try one of these substantial salads. All you need to make a meal of it is some good bread or rolls; add an easy ice cream dessert (see pages 121–123) if you wish.

SMOKED TURKEY SALAD

Easily assembled, this salad combines turkey with cheese, fresh vegetables, and a tangy sour-cream dressing.

> ¾ *pound smoked turkey, cut into thin strips*
> ¼ *pound jack cheese, cut into thin strips*
> 1¼ *cups cooked fresh peas, or frozen petit peas, thawed but not cooked*
> ⅓ *cup diced red bell pepper or 2 tablespoons diced pimiento*
> 2 *tablespoons chopped chives or 2 small green onions, sliced*
> ⅓ *cup mayonnaise*
> ⅓ *cup sour cream*
> 1½ *to 2 tablespoons prepared horseradish*
> *Freshly ground pepper to taste*

1. In a large bowl toss together turkey, cheese, peas, bell pepper, and chives.

2. In a separate bowl blend mayonnaise, sour cream, and horseradish.

3. Add dressing to turkey mixture; gently toss to coat. Season liberally with pepper.

Serves 5 to 6.

Preparation Time About 15 minutes

Luncheon on the patio: Invite friends in to enjoy a sunny afternoon over Smoked Turkey Salad served with a dry white wine such as a Riesling or a Chardonnay.

1. In a small bowl combine beans, onions, capers, caper juice, and ¼ cup of Mild Vinaigrette.

2. In a separate bowl combine tuna and ¼ cup of Mild Vinaigrette.

3. Line 4 individual serving plates with salad greens. Arrange a mound of bean-onion mixture and a mound of tuna in the center of the plate.

4. Arrange tomato wedges, cucumber slices, olives, and anchovy fillets (if used) on the plates.

5. Pass remaining vinaigrette at the table.

Serves 4.

Preparation Time 20 to 25 minutes

MENDOCINO SALAD

A great way to use up leftover chicken or turkey.

> 3 cups shredded cooked chicken or turkey, loosely packed
> 1 cup halved seedless grapes
> 1 green onion, chopped
> ⅔ cup toasted slivered almonds or toasted unsalted cashews
> 2 tablespoons each mayonnaise and sour cream
> 2 teaspoons lemon juice
> ¾ teaspoon minced fresh dill or tarragon or ⅛ to ¼ teaspoon dried
> Salt and freshly ground pepper to taste
> Salad greens

1. In a medium mixing bowl combine shredded chicken, grapes, green onion, and ½ cup of the nuts. Reserve remaining nuts.

2. In a small mixing bowl stir together mayonnaise, sour cream, lemon juice, and dill.

3. Fold mayonnaise mixture into chicken mixture. Season with salt and pepper to taste.

This full-meal salad brings the flavors of southern France to your table. It features tuna, beans, and fresh vegetables, accented with anchovies and Niçoise olives.

LAURA'S COMPOSED SALAD

This salad is similar to a salade Niçoise, but it's a bit easier than the classic because there are no potatoes, eggs, or green beans to cook.

> 1 can (16 oz) white beans, drained
> ¼ cup chopped red or green onion
> 1½ teaspoons capers plus 2 to 3 teaspoons caper juice
> Mild Vinaigrette (see opposite page)
> 1 can (12 oz) tuna packed in water, drained
> Salad greens
> 1 large tomato, cut into wedges
> 20 thin cucumber slices
> 12 Niçoise olives or whole pitted ripe olives
> 4 anchovy fillets, rolled or flat (optional)

4. Serve on salad greens, garnished with remaining nuts.

Serves 4 to 6.

Preparation Time 15 to 20 minutes

Timesaver Tip If the salad is prepared ahead, reserve all the nuts. Mix the ½ cup in just before serving, to prevent their getting soggy.

BOMBAY TUNA

This sweet-and-tangy mix—tuna combined with apple, currants, and almonds and flavored with mustard and curry powder—is equally good as a salad or as a sandwich.

> 1 can (6½ oz) tuna packed in water, well drained
> ½ cup cubed unpeeled apple (pippin or other tart variety)
> ⅓ cup diced celery
> 1 green onion, sliced
> ¼ cup slivered almonds or coarsely chopped toasted almonds
> 2 tablespoons currants
> ¼ cup mayonnaise
> 2 teaspoons chutney, finely chopped
> 1½ teaspoons Dijon mustard
> ½ teaspoon curry powder, or to taste

1. In a medium bowl, combine tuna, apple, celery, green onion, almonds, and currants.

2. Stir in mayonnaise, chutney, mustard, and curry powder.

Makes 3 salads or 4 sandwiches.

Preparation Time About 15 minutes

A QUARTET OF VINAIGRETTES

Here's a basic vinaigrette plus three variations—a choice for almost any salad. The Mild Vinaigrette has a touch of sugar for a slightly sweeter dressing. The Creamy Vinaigrette, with mustard for zestiness and whipping cream as a luscious thickener, makes a nice partner to butter lettuce. The Grapefruit Vinaigrette is light and refreshing, and low in calories as well. It's particularly good with tossed greens. Any of the dressings can be made in the food processor: Fit it with the steel blade, add all ingredients at once, and process for 3 seconds.

BASIC VINAIGRETTE

> 1 tablespoon Dijon mustard
> 3 tablespoons vinegar or lemon juice
> ½ cup olive oil or vegetable oil, or a combination Salt and pepper to taste

In a small bowl whisk together mustard, vinegar, and oil. Taste and add salt and pepper to taste. Whisk again to blend well.

Makes about ¾ cup.

Preparation Time About 5 minutes

Timesaver Tip Dressing can be prepared ahead and kept up to 2 weeks, covered, in the refrigerator.

MILD VINAIGRETTE

> ¼ cup white wine vinegar
> 2 tablespoons Dijon mustard
> 1 teaspoon sugar
> ¾ cup olive oil or vegetable oil

In a bowl, combine vinegar, mustard, and sugar. Whisk in oil.

Makes 1 cup.

CREAMY VINAIGRETTE

> 3 tablespoons light olive oil
> 1 tablespoon white wine vinegar
> ½ teaspoon Dijon mustard
> 2 tablespoons whipping cream

In a small bowl, whisk together oil, vinegar, and mustard. Add cream; whisk vigorously until well blended.

Makes ⅓ cup.

GRAPEFRUIT VINAIGRETTE

> ½ cup fresh grapefruit juice
> 6 to 7 tablespoons balsamic vinegar (see Note)
> ⅓ cup peanut oil or vegetable oil
> 2½ tablespoons sesame oil
> 2 tablespoons Dijon mustard

1. In a small bowl whisk together grapefruit juice, vinegar, peanut oil, sesame oil, and mustard. Chill slightly.

2. Pour dressing over salad and toss to coat.

Makes 1½ cups.

Preparation Time About 5 minutes

Timesaver Tip Dressing can be made up to 1 week ahead and stored, covered, in refrigerator.

Note The mild balsamic vinegar makes a difference. Rice wine vinegar and cider vinegar are suitable alternatives; if you must use wine vinegar, decrease the amount to taste.

A WORLD OF OILS AND VINEGARS

A wide spectrum of oils and vinegars is now available in supermarkets and specialty food shops.
Balsamic vinegar is intensely aromatic and flavorful; it is delicious on tomato salads.
Cider vinegar gives an apple tartness to sweet fruit salads and well-seasoned dressings.
Red and white wine vinegars are subtle. Use white in delicate salads and red in heartier ones.
Sherry vinegar, slightly sweet, blends well with fruit or cheese salads.
Rice vinegar, fermented sake, gives a sweet-sour taste to Oriental salads.
Fruit vinegars such as raspberry, blueberry, and peach offer a fresh, flowery bouquet for leafy salads.
Herb vinegars—basil, tarragon, mint, thyme, and burnet—have faint herb flavoring.
Olive oils, in order of quality: extra-virgin has a fruity or peppery taste; virgin is lightly fruity or sweet and nutty; pure has a faint olive flavor; fine is best used for frying.
Nut and seed oils: walnut, hazelnut, grape seed, and sesame seed are rich and nutty; peanut, safflower, and sunflower seed are lighter.
Vegetable oil is too heavy for salads.

SIDE-DISH SALADS

Side-dish salads are accompaniments to a dinner or perhaps part of a soup or sandwich lunch. They provide an opportunity to balance the meal in terms of flavors, textures, colors, and nutritional profile. The selection here includes hot and spicy Szechwan Sprout Salad (see page 103), colorful Roasted Pepper Salad (see page 103), and two vegetable salads, one of which offers a protein boost to the meal (Garbanzo, Feta, and Tomato Salad, page 103).

HERBED PEA SALAD

Young and tender home-grown peas are particularly nice in this recipe. You may use either dill or mint, but they are very nice together.

> 2 packages (10 oz each) frozen tiny peas, or 4 cups fresh peas
> 2 tablespoons mayonnaise
> 2 tablespoons sour cream
> 2 teaspoons lemon juice
> 1 to 2 tablespoons finely chopped fresh dill or ¾ to 1 teaspoon dried
> 2 to 4 teaspoons finely chopped mint (do not use dried)

1. Thaw peas and pat dry with paper towels. (Peas can be thawed in the microwave oven on Defrost setting for 3 to 4 minutes.)

2. In a small bowl, mix together mayonnaise, sour cream, lemon juice, and herbs.

3. Just before serving, mix together dressing and peas.

Serves 6 to 8.

SALAD OF PEARS, ROQUEFORT, AND WALNUTS

An intriguing combination of flavors and textures, this salad is a refreshing accompaniment to a dinner featuring roast meat of any kind.

> 5 to 6 cups loosely packed torn mixed salad greens (any combination of butter, red leaf, or oak leaf lettuce, romaine, watercress, radicchio, or arugula)
> 2 ounces (⅓ to ½ cup) crumbled Roquefort (see Note)
> ½ cup broken walnut pieces, toasted
> 1 large, firm pear

Sherry Dressing

> 3½ tablespoons hazelnut oil, peanut oil, or vegetable oil
> 1 tablespoon plus 1 teaspoon sherry vinegar
> Pinch sugar
> Salt and freshly ground pepper to taste

1. Prepare Sherry Dressing.

2. In a large bowl, toss together salad greens, Roquefort, and walnuts.

3. Peel, halve, and core pear; cut in julienne strips, thinly slice, or cube. Add to greens.

4. Toss salad with Sherry Dressing and serve.

Serves 5 to 6.

Sherry Dressing In a small bowl whisk together oil, vinegar, and sugar. Add salt and pepper to taste.

Preparation Time About 15 minutes

Timesaver Tip Recipe ingredients can be prepared ahead and the salad tossed with dressing just before serving. To keep cut pears from discoloring, rub surfaces with lemon juice.

Note Gorgonzola or blue cheese can be substituted for the Roquefort.

LEAFY SALADS

A leafy salad serves either as an appetizer, awaking one's taste for delights to come, or as a palate refresher after the entrée. For either purpose, a multitude of greens, herbs, and even flowers may be combined in infinite variety.

When it comes to selecting and combining greens, simplicity should reign, but never without imagination. Choose from among many options of taste and appearance. Romaine and iceberg lettuce give crispness, butter and oak leaf lettuce contribute softness and interesting shapes, and the color of red leaf lettuce or radicchio brightens the mixture. A few shredded leaves of sorrel lend a pleasant tartness; curly endive adds texture and and interesting bitterness. There's a sharp bite to watercress, arugula, Belgian endive, and dandelion leaves, while spinach has a coarse texture.

The addition of herbs and flowers expands the range even more. Nasturtiums, chrysanthemums, violas, violets, alyssum, daylilies, roses, and dianthus are just a few of the edible flowers that you can use, as long as they are free of chemical sprays. Herb flowers add lovely flavor and color. The flavors of the herbs themselves are intense, so use them judiciously.

In many restaurants today, chefs are combining the salad and cheese courses. If you plan to serve salad after the main dish, it's a nice touch to add a few shavings of Parmesan cheese, a small piece of goat cheese, or a sliver of Brie to the plate.

Leafy salads need only a simple vinaigrette dressing to anoint the leaves. The type and proportion of vinegar or lemon juice and oil can be varied to suit the salad. For example, a salad of delicate greens calls for a mild dressing with a smaller proportion of acid—perhaps a rasp-

berry or rice vinegar—and a mild olive, vegetable, or nut oil, whereas assertive greens could support a dressing made with stronger-flavored oils and vinegars.

The standard proportions for a vinaigrette are 1 part acid to 3 parts oil. To that, one can add Dijon mustard or minced garlic. Use only enough dressing to lightly coat the greens, about 2 tablespoons per cup of leaves. Mix the dressing with the greens just before serving.

Experiment with a wide range of edible plants for a salad that's interesting and beautiful as well as tasty. The elements of the salad above include violets, rose petals, rosemary blossoms, chicory, arugula, nasturtium, and mâche. To obtain these more unusual salad makings, it's best to grow your own or to buy from a specialty store, in order to be sure that they are free of the chemical sprays often used on ornamental plants.

Delicious Roasted Pepper Salad can be made up to a day ahead. The dish is great for a buffet, or take it to a potluck or a picnic.

SZECHWAN SPROUT SALAD

A hot and spicy salad; control just how hot by the amount of red pepper flakes you put in.

- ½ pound mung bean sprouts
- 2 tablespoons rice wine vinegar
- 1 tablespoon soy sauce
- .2 teaspoons sesame oil
- ½ teaspoon sugar
- ⅛ to ¼ teaspoon crushed red pepper flakes
- 3 tablespoons thinly sliced green onion

1. Rinse sprouts and pat dry with paper towels.

2. In a small bowl stir together vinegar, soy sauce, sesame oil, sugar, and red pepper flakes.

3. In a serving bowl combine sprouts and onion. Pour dressing over and toss to coat.

Serves 3 to 4.

Preparation Time About 15 minutes

Timesaver Tip Recipe tastes as good, if not better, when made up to 4 hours in advance. Store, covered, in refrigerator and serve either chilled or at room temperature.

ROASTED PEPPER SALAD

This colorful salad is delicious, and also convenient, since it is served at room temperature.

- 4 red bell peppers, or a combination of red, green, and yellow peppers
- ⅓ cup olive oil
- 2 tablespoons balsamic vinegar or red wine vinegar
- 2 to 3 tablespoons finely chopped fresh parsley, basil, or a combination of herbs
- 1 clove garlic, minced

1. Roast peppers over an open flame or in broiler, turning frequently, until skins are charred and blistered. Place in a plastic bag; close top and let sit 5 to 10 minutes. Remove skins under running water.

2. Cut peppers in half, holding them over a bowl to catch juice. Remove seeds and stem. Tear lengthwise into strips ½ to 1 inch wide. Put in a serving bowl or dish.

3. In a small bowl whisk together pepper juice, olive oil, vinegar, herbs, and garlic. Pour over peppers.

4. Serve immediately or marinate at room temperature several hours.

Serves 6 to 8.

Preparation Time About 30 minutes

Timesaver Tip Recipe can be made up to 1 day ahead. Store in the refrigerator, covered. Serve at room temperature.

GARBANZO, FETA, AND TOMATO SALAD

This is a tasty filling for pita sandwiches, too.

- 1 can (15½ oz) garbanzo beans, drained
- ½ cup crumbled feta cheese (about 3 oz)
- 1 large tomato, seeded and diced (about 1 cup)
- 2 green onions, sliced
- 2 tablespoons finely chopped parsley
- 1½ tablespoons olive oil
- 2 to 3 teaspoons red wine vinegar
  Freshly ground pepper to taste

1. Place garbanzo beans, feta, tomato, onions, and parsley in a bowl; toss gently to combine.

2. In a small bowl whisk together olive oil and vinegar. Pour over salad, tossing gently to coat. Season to taste with pepper.

Serves 4 to 6.

Preparation Time 10 to 15 minutes

Variation Add herbs, such as thyme and oregano, and Greek olives or pitted black ripe olives.

Menu

A SALAD BUFFET

Oriental Pasta Salad

*Mendocino Salad
(see page 98)*

*Salad of Pears,
Roquefort, and Walnuts
(see page 100)*

*Sliced Tomatoes
With Olives*

*Cheese Platter
With Bread*

Chilled White Wine

---

*For luncheon on a
summer day, offer
guests a light
but filling buffet of
salads. The Oriental
Pasta Salad and
Mendocino Salad
can be made the day
before; keep
refrigerated until
serving time. The
morning of the
party, prepare the
pear salad and slice
the season's ripest,
most flavorful
tomatoes (serve with
just olive oil and
vinegar).*

ORIENTAL PASTA SALAD

This pasta salad is refreshing on a warm summer day. The crisp vegetables and soft tortellini are a wonderful combination.

2 packages (12 oz each) frozen tortellini
4 to 6 tablespoons rice vinegar
3 to 3½ tablespoons soy sauce
1 large clove garlic, minced
2 tablespoons minced fresh ginger
1½ teaspoons sugar
¾ teaspoon dried hot red pepper flakes
¾ teaspoon dry mustard
¼ teaspoon Five Spice powder
¼ cup sesame oil
½ large red bell pepper, finely diced
⅓ cup chopped green onions
2 to 3 ounces snow peas, cut diagonally (to make about ⅔ cup)
1 medium carrot, cut into 2-inch julienne strips
Chinese (Nappa) cabbage or spinach leaves

1. Cook tortellini according to package directions. Drain well and place in a large bowl.

2. Combine 4 tablespoons vinegar, 3 tablespoons soy sauce, garlic, ginger, sugar, red pepper flakes, dry mustard, and Five Spice powder in a small bowl. Whisk in oil.

3. Toss warm tortellini with dressing. Toss in red bell pepper, green onion, snow peas, and carrot. Add more vinegar and soy sauce to taste, if desired.

4. Line a serving platter or individual serving plates with cabbage or spinach leaves. Arrange salad over greens. Serve at room temperature.

Serves 4 to 6.

Preparation Time About 30 minutes

Timesaver Tip Recipe can be made up to 1 day ahead and refrigerated. Bring to room temperature before serving.

Salads for a summer day (front to rear): Mendocino Salad, Oriental Pasta Salad, Salad of Pears, Roquefort, and Walnuts, sliced tomatoes with olives.

SIDE DISHES

Tastes in food are always changing; no longer is dinner inevitably meat and potatoes. For an alternative side dish, try the recipes in this section. Most of them cook themselves in a covered pot, freeing the cook to prepare other dishes. These filling dishes complete the menu, and, eaten in moderation, they're not high-calorie.

HOMEMADE SPAETZLE

These fresh homemade noodles are surprisingly easy and quick to make. A metal spaetzle maker, which looks like a strainer with ¼-inch-diameter holes, is handy to have. (They're inexpensive and can be found in cookware shops.) However, in a pinch, you can force the spaetzle batter through a flat cheese grater or a colander with large holes.

    8 cups water
    2 cups flour
    ¼ teaspoon salt
    ¼ teaspoon ground nutmeg
    3 eggs, lightly beaten
       About ¾ cup milk
       Butter or margarine to taste

1. Bring the water to a boil.

2. Meanwhile, combine flour, salt, and nutmeg in a mixing bowl.

3. Stir in eggs and gradually add enough milk to make a heavy batter.

4. Force some of the batter through the holes of a spaetzle maker or colander into the boiling water. The spaetzle will cook quickly. As they rise to the surface, remove them with a slotted spoon to a colander. Rinse spaetzle with cold water and drain. Repeat until batter is used up.

5. Traditionally, spaetzle is sautéed in butter until golden brown. It's also good simply tossed with a little butter.

Serves 4 to 6.

Preparation Time 20 to 25 minutes

MELON SEED PASTA

Orzo, available today in most supermarkets, is also called melon seed pasta because of its shape.

       Salted water
    ¾ cup orzo
    1 tablespoon butter
    2 tablespoons finely chopped parsley
       Freshly ground pepper to taste

1. In a large saucepan bring about 1½ quarts of salted water to a boil. Add orzo and cook 8 to 12 minutes, or until done. Drain.

2. Toss pasta with butter and parsley. Season with pepper. Serve immediately.

Serves 4.

Preparation Time About 15 minutes

BULGUR PILAF

Bulgur is gaining popularity with cooks in this country. It is a good counterpoint to sharply flavored dishes such as Lamb with Mint Vinaigrette (see page 73).

    1 teaspoon butter or margarine
    ¼ cup finely chopped onion
    ½ cup bulgur
    1 cup homemade chicken or beef stock or canned chicken broth, preferably low-sodium
    1 tablespoon finely chopped parsley
       Salt and freshly ground pepper to taste

1. In a medium saucepan over medium heat, melt butter. Add onion and cook until soft and translucent.

2. Stir in bulgur and broth. Cover pan. Bring to a boil; reduce heat and simmer 15 minutes or until liquid has been absorbed.

3. Stir in parsley. Season to taste with salt and pepper.

Serves 3 to 4.

Preparation Time About 20 minutes

GINGER RICE

An excellent accompaniment to chicken, fish, or pork. It will reheat beautifully in the microwave oven.

    2 cups water
    2 tablespoons vermouth or dry white wine
    1½ tablespoons minced fresh ginger
    1 tablespoon butter or margarine
    ½ teaspoon salt
    1 cup long-grain white rice

1. In a small, heavy saucepan combine the water, vermouth, ginger, butter, and salt. Bring to a boil, reduce heat to low, and stir in rice.

2. Cover saucepan and cook for 15 to 20 minutes, or until all the liquid is absorbed. Toss gently with a fork before serving.

Serves 4 to 5.

Preparation Time About 25 minutes

PECAN RICE

This dish will reheat well in the microwave oven.

- 1 tablespoon butter or margarine
- ⅔ cup finely chopped onion
- ⅓ cup chopped pecans
- 1 cup long-grain rice
- 2 cups homemade chicken stock or 1 can (10½ oz) chicken broth, preferably low-sodium, plus water to make 2 cups
- ½ teaspoon dried basil
  Salt and freshly ground pepper to taste

1. In a medium saucepan over medium heat, melt butter. Add onions and pecans and sauté until pecans are toasted, about 5 minutes.

2. Add rice. Stir in stock and basil.

3. Cover and cook until liquid is absorbed, 18 to 20 minutes. Remove from heat; let stand 5 minutes.

4. Toss rice gently with a fork and season to taste with salt and pepper.

Serves 4 to 6.

Preparation Time About 25 minutes

A traditional favorite of German cuisine, spaetzle are nutmeg-scented morsels of dough, quickly boiled and then sautéed until golden in butter.

Fresh fruit is the starting point for a wide variety of desserts, from sautéed compotes and tangy sorbets to toppings and sauces.

Fast & Fabulous Desserts

Everybody likes dessert, but sometimes it seems there's no time to make anything special. With the help of timesaving appliances, however, you can easily satisfy the sweet tooth. In this chapter you'll find recipes for chocolate desserts (pages 110–112); fresh fruit desserts (pages 114–117); sauces and toppings to go on ice cream, fruit, or cake (pages 118–120); and ice creams, sorbets, and frosty desserts (pages 121–123)— all quickly made and sure to be a hit.

Truffle Cups make a smashing impression filled with fresh fruit, ice cream, or chocolate mousse. You might also try raspberry Fresh Fruit Sorbet (see page 123) or Easy and Elegant Lemon Mousse (see page 114).

CHOCOLATE DESSERTS

The desserts in this section are all treats for the chocophile that can be made quickly using the microwave oven and other timesaving appliances.

CHOCOLATE MADNESS

You'll love the silken texture of this dessert. Other flavorings can be substituted for the mint, or it can be left out entirely.

> 1 cup whipping cream
> ½ cup unsalted butter or margarine, at room temperature
> 1 package (6 oz) semisweet chocolate chips
> 4 egg yolks
> ¼ to ½ teaspoon mint extract, or other flavoring to taste
> Mint leaves or whipped cream for decoration (optional)

1. Bring cream to a boil in a small, heavy saucepan.

2. Cut butter into chunks. Put butter, chocolate chips, egg yolks, and mint extract in bowl of food processor or blender; add hot cream. Process until smooth (about 30 seconds). Adjust flavoring to taste.

3. Pour mixture into small dessert dishes and chill in freezer about 45 minutes, or in refrigerator for several hours. Decorate with mint leaves or whipped cream, if desired.

Makes 6 servings, ½ cup each.

Preparation Time 8 to 10 minutes

Timesaver Tip Recipe can be prepared up to a day ahead and stored, covered, in refrigerator.

Microwave Version

Pour cream into a glass bowl or 2-cup glass measure. Microwave on 100% power until tiny bubbles break the surface (2 to 3 minutes). Continue with step 2. Preparation time and timesaver tips same as above.

TRUFFLE CUPS

Simple and quick to make, Truffle Cups make appealing containers for ice cream and sorbet, or fruit such as strawberries. For a chocolate splurge, fill them with Chocolate Madness (see page 110) or Mousse in Minutes (see page 112). Each Truffle Cup holds about ⅓ cup filling.

1. Melt 6 ounces finely chopped semisweet chocolate or 1 package (6 oz) semisweet chocolate chips in a double boiler or a bowl set over a pan of hot water. Stir until smooth.

2. Working quickly, use the back of a spoon or a small knife to spread chocolate on bottom and up sides of 6 to 8 paper cupcake liners. Set liners in a muffin pan. Chill until firm in freezer, 10 to 15 minutes, or in refrigerator 20 to 30 minutes. Carefully peel off the paper liners, handling chocolate as little as possible.

Makes 6 to 8 Truffle Cups.

Preparation Time 15 to 20 minutes

Timesaver Tip Recipe can be prepared up to 5 days ahead. Store Truffle Cups in the refrigerator, tightly wrapped in plastic wrap to prevent moisture condensation. After a number of days, the Truffle Cups *may* develop a grayish tinge, caused by cocoa butter rising to the surface. The chocolate may be less attractive, but it will be no less flavorful or safe to eat.

Microwave Version

Chocolate may be melted in the microwave oven. Place chocolate in a small glass bowl. Microwave on 50% power until softened (2 to 2½ minutes). Stir until smooth. Do not overheat or chocolate will scorch around edges and won't blend smoothly. Continue with step 2. Preparation time and timesaver tip same as above.

ORANGE-SCENTED CHOCOLATE SAUCE

Serve a pool of this rich sauce topped with fresh fruit such as strawberries, bananas, peaches, or pears. It's also good with ice cream or a rich fruit *sorbet* (sherbet). Double the recipe and you'll have a terrific chocolate fondue.

- *4 tablespoons unsalted butter or margarine*
- *4 ounces sweet baking chocolate, broken into pieces*
- *1 to 2 tablespoons freshly squeezed orange juice*
- *¼ to ½ teaspoon finely grated orange rind*

1. Melt butter in heavy saucepan. Add chocolate and stir until smooth.

2. Stir in orange juice and rind, adjusting to taste.

Makes ½ cup sauce (4 to 6 servings).

Preparation Time 5 to 8 minutes

Timesaver Tip Recipe can be prepared up to 5 days ahead and stored, covered, in refrigerator. Gently reheat in a saucepan or in a microwave oven.

Microwave Version

Place butter and chocolate in a small glass bowl. Microwave on 50% power for 1 minute, stir, then microwave 1 to 3 minutes more. Stir in orange juice and rind. Preparation time and timesaver tip same as above.

HANDLING CHOCOLATE

Melting Chocolate burns easily, so always use low heat. Melt chocolate in a heatproof cup or in the top of double boiler, set over barely simmering water. Or, microwave at 50% power (2 to 5 minutes for 1 or 2 squares, 3 to 5 minutes for 1 cup chips), stirring every 2 minutes. When melting it with liquid or fat, use a heavy saucepan set over low flame. Moisture in the pan will cause chocolate to "seize" or harden. (Add 1 teaspoon shortening per ounce of chocolate to restore smoothness.) When working with melted chocolate (as for Truffle Cups at left), work quickly. Warm fingers melt the chocolate; dip them in ice water (then dry them) as you work.*

Whitening If you exceed chocolate's ideal storage temperature of 78° F, some of the cocoa butter will rise to the surface as a whitish "fat bloom." There is nothing wrong with whitened chocolate; melting will restore the color.*

Curls Using long, thin strokes, shave the sides or bottom of a warm cube of sweet or semisweet chocolate with a swivel-bladed vegetable parer or a thin, sharp knife. Position curls on the dessert with a wooden toothpick.*

PRESTO POTS DE CRÈME

These are sinfully rich yet not too sweet. Since this recipe serves eight, and can be prepared in advance, it's great for entertaining.

- *7 ounces unsweetened chocolate*
- *1 can (14 oz) sweetened condensed milk*
- *3 tablespoons or more orange liqueur*
- *1½ cups whipping cream, whipped until soft peaks form*

1. Heat chocolate and sweetened condensed milk in double boiler or a bowl set over a pan of hot water. Stir until chocolate melts and mixture is blended.

2. Stir in liqueur, adjusting to taste, and let mixture cool to lukewarm. Stir about a fourth of whipped cream into chocolate to lighten mixture. Then fold in all but one large spoonful of remaining whipped cream. Refrigerate remaining cream to decorate tops.

3. Spoon mixture into *pots-de-crème* pots, individual soufflé cups, or small dessert dishes. Chill in freezer about 30 minutes, or in refrigerator if serving time is more than 30 minutes away. Decorate each dessert with a dollop of reserved whipped cream.

Makes 8 servings, ½ cup each.

Preparation Time About 20 minutes

Timesaver Tip Recipe can be prepared up to a day ahead and stored, covered, in refrigerator.

Microwave Version

Chocolate may be melted in the microwave oven. Place chocolate in a small glass bowl. Microwave on 50% power until softened (2 to 2½ minutes). Stir until smooth. Do not overheat or chocolate will scorch around edges and won't blend smoothly. Add sweetened condensed milk, stir to blend, and continue with step 2. Preparation time and timesaver tip same as above.

AMARETTO CHOCOLATE SAUCE

This is a heavenly sauce for ice cream.

- *½ cup whipping cream*
- *½ pound semisweet chocolate, chopped, or 1⅓ cups (8 oz) semisweet chocolate chips*
- *1 tablespoon amaretto or other liqueur*

1. Bring cream to a simmer in a small saucepan. Remove from heat.

2. Stir in chocolate until it is melted and mixture is smooth.

3. Stir in liqueur.

Makes 1¼ cups.

Preparation Time 8 to 10 minutes

Timesaver Tip Recipe can be prepared up to 4 days ahead and stored, covered, in refrigerator. Gently reheat in a saucepan or in a microwave oven.

Microwave Version

1. Pour cream into a glass bowl or 2-cup measure. Microwave on 100% power until tiny bubbles break the surface (1 to 2 minutes).

2. Stir in chocolate until it is melted and mixture is smooth. If chocolate does not melt completely, microwave on 100% power until it is completely melted (20 to 30 seconds longer).

3. Stir in liqueur.

Preparation Time 3 to 5 minutes

Timesaver Tip Same as above.

MOUSSE IN MINUTES

This is a light mocha mousse that can be prepared in no time. To make chocolate mousse, simply leave out the instant coffee. Sifting the powdered sugar and cocoa removes any lumps and ensures a velvety smooth mousse.

- *1⅓ cups whipping cream*
- *⅔ cup confectioners' sugar, sifted*
- *⅓ cup Dutch-process cocoa, sifted (see Note)*
- *1 teaspoon or more powdered instant coffee (not granules)*
- *2 teaspoons or more dark rum (optional)*
- *Confectioners' sugar or cocoa, for decoration*

1. Place cream, sugar, cocoa, instant coffee, and rum (if used) in large mixing bowl. Beat with electric mixer or whisk until cream forms soft peaks but is not stiff. Adjust flavoring to taste.

2. Spoon into small dessert dishes and refrigerate until serving. Decorate tops with a dusting of confectioners' sugar or cocoa, if desired, just before serving.

Serves 4. Mousse will fill 6 to 8 Truffle Cups, page 111.

Preparation Time 8 to 10 minutes

Timesaver Tip Recipe can be prepared up to a day ahead and stored, covered, in refrigerator.

Note Dutch-process cocoa (or "dutched cocoa") has been treated with a mild alkali, such as baking soda, to neutralize the natural acids present. The alkali modifies the flavor and darkens the color. Dutch-process cocoa is available at supermarkets, but any unsweetened cocoa powder may be used.

The classic recipe for French pots de crème produces a baked custard. This quick version, which is lightened with whipped cream, is more like a mousse.

FRESH FRUIT DESSERTS

It's all too easy for a busy cook to resort to dessert from a mix or a commercial frozen product. But for optimum flavor and food quality, to say nothing of the special touch that something homemade has, the made-from-scratch dessert can't be beat. In addition, most prepared food has calories and additives the careful cook prefers to avoid. To the rescue: the desserts in this section, based on healthful fruit and designed to take advantage of timesaving appliances such as the microwave oven, electric mixer, and food processor.

WARM SAUTÉ OF SUMMER FRUIT

Use any combination of fresh fruit that looks beautiful together: grapes, cherries, berries, peaches, plums, nectarines, bananas. For a low-calorie dessert, serve as is; or serve with Crème Fraîche (see page 118) or whipped cream .

- 1½ tablespoons unsalted butter or margarine
- 1½ tablespoons sugar
- 1 cup sliced strawberries or pitted Bing cherries
- ¾ cup blueberries
- 1 cup sliced peaches, nectarines, peeled kiwi, or other fresh fruit
- 1 to 2 tablespoons kirsch or 1 teaspoon orange liqueur (to taste)

1. Melt butter in a sauté pan or large skillet. Stir in sugar.

2. Add fresh fruits and liqueur. Adjust liqueur to taste.

3. Cook over medium heat, basting with sauce, until fruits are warmed through. Do not overcook.

Serves 4 to 6.

Preparation Time 8 to 10 minutes

EASY AND ELEGANT LEMON MOUSSE

Serve this light and refreshing citrus dessert after a hearty dinner, or as a counterpoint to a spicy meal such as curry. For a variation, you can substitute lime juice and rind for the lemon.

- 2½ teaspoons finely grated lemon rind (1 lemon)
- 1 cup whipping cream
- ¼ cup sugar
- 3 tablespoons lemon juice

1. Chill bowl and beaters for electric mixer in freezer until ready to use.

2. Reserve ½ teaspoon of the grated lemon rind. In chilled bowl, whip remaining ingredients until light and fluffy.

3. Serve in stemmed glasses or individual soufflé dishes. Garnish with remaining grated lemon rind.

Makes 4 servings, ½ cup each.

Preparation Time 10 to 15 minutes

Timesaver Tip Recipe can be prepared up to a day ahead and stored, covered, in refrigerator. If you make it more than an hour prior to serving, add 1 tablespoon sweetened condensed milk, which will stabilize the mousse and keep it from weeping.

Variation Prepare mousse using lime instead of lemon. Halve and seed two papayas, fluting edges. Using a pastry bag fitted with a star tip, pipe mousse into papaya halves. Garnish with lime slices.

BANANAS NEW ORLEANS

A rich brown-sugar sauce turns bananas into a marvelous topping for ice cream or pound cake.

- 2 tablespoons butter or margarine
- 3 tablespoons brown sugar
- ¼ cup orange juice
- 1 tablespoon dark rum (optional)
- ⅛ teaspoon or more ground cinnamon
- 2 bananas
  Ice cream or pound cake

1. Melt butter in a medium skillet. Stir in brown sugar, orange juice, rum (if used), and cinnamon. Bring to a boil; cook and stir over medium-high heat for several minutes, or until mixture is reduced by about one quarter. Sauce will be slightly syrupy.

2. Peel bananas, split in half lengthwise, then cut into 1½-inch pieces, or slice bananas crosswise into 1-inch chunks. Add bananas to sauce in pan. Cook bananas just enough to heat through, basting with sauce. Do not overcook, or bananas will be mushy.

3. Spoon bananas and sauce over ice cream or cake. Serve immediately.

Serves 4.

Preparation Time 10 to 15 minutes

Timesaver Tip Recipe can be prepared up to 4 hours ahead. Just before serving, reheat sauce and add bananas.

Variation Split 3 bananas lengthwise, then cut in half. Follow directions above, adding 2 tablespoons whipping cream or half-and-half along with ingredients in step 1. Arrange 3 banana slices per serving on dessert plates. Spoon on sauce. Garnish with mint sprig.

Microwave Version

1. Place butter in a 9- or 10-inch glass pie plate. Microwave on 100% power 30 to 45 seconds to melt. Stir in brown sugar, orange juice, rum (if used), and cinnamon. Microwave on 100% power 2 to 3 minutes, or until mixture is reduced by about one quarter. Stir once during cooking. Sauce will be slightly syrupy.

2. Meanwhile, peel bananas. Split lengthwise, then cut into 1½-inch pieces, or slice bananas crosswise into 1-inch chunks. Add bananas to sauce, spooning sauce over bananas to baste. Microwave on 100% power 30 to 45 seconds, just to heat bananas through. Do not overcook, or bananas will be mushy.

3. Spoon bananas and sauce over ice cream or cake. Serve immediately. Preparation time and timesaver tip same as above.

WARM SAUTÉ OF WINTER FRUIT

This fruit combination is wonderful with yogurt, ice cream, or Crème Fraîche (see page 118).

> 2 tablespoons butter or margarine
> 1½ to 2 tablespoons maple syrup
> 1 large apple, cored and thinly sliced
> 1 firm, ripe pear, cored and thinly sliced
> ⅓ cup raisins or currants
> ⅓ cup chopped walnuts or pecans
>   Dash each ground cinnamon and nutmeg
> 2 tablespoons water
> 1 to 2 tablespoons brandy

1. Melt butter in a sauté pan or large skillet. Stir in maple syrup and adjust to taste.

2. Add remaining ingredients. Cook over medium heat and stir until fruits are tender.

Serves 4 to 6.

Preparation Time 15 to 20 minutes

Timesaver Tip Ingredients can be prepared ahead; rub apple and pear slices with lemon juice to prevent browning.

Easy and Elegant Lemon Mousse, an airy chilled dessert that contrasts the tang of citrus with the smoothness of whipped cream, can be made up to a day ahead.

For a spectacular dessert in the nouvelle style, steam fresh pears, then serve in a pool of Raspberry Sauce patterned with Crème Fraîche.

STEAMED PEARS NOUVELLE

When steamed, pears retain their natural flavor and sweetness, and they cook quickly. This is a beautiful dessert, and relatively low in calories, as well.

> 2 large pears
> Lemon juice
> Raspberry Sauce (see page 118)
> ¼ cup plain low-fat yogurt or Crème Fraîche (see page 118)
> Thin slivers of orange rind
> Mint leaves (optional)

1. Peel, halve, and core pears. Rub with lemon juice to prevent browning.

2. Place pear halves, cut side down, on steamer rack. Steam until tender; check by piercing with a knife tip. Steaming time varies considerably depending on pear variety and ripeness. Check after 5 minutes.

3. Cool to room temperature, then refrigerate to chill.

4. Prepare Raspberry Sauce.

5. Place yogurt or Crème Fraîche in a pastry bag fitted with a fine tip, or in a squeeze-type plastic mustard or ketchup bottle.

6. Ladle about ¼ cup Raspberry Sauce on each of 4 dessert plates.

7. Pipe yogurt in a spiral design on sauce. Draw a knife from the center of the plate, spoke fashion, to create a web design (or make other designs—use your imagination).

8. Place a chilled pear half, cut side down, on sauce.

9. Arrange thin slivers of orange rind on pear. Garnish plates with mint, if desired.

Serves 4.

Preparation Time About 30 minutes

Timesaver Tip Pears can be steamed and Raspberry Sauce made up to a day ahead. Assemble dessert just before serving.

COCONUT-CREAM CLOUDS

Rich with cream cheese, this dessert is whipped for lightness and then chilled. The delicate dish that results is particularly appropriate to finish off a spicy meal. It's flavored with coconut snow and cream of coconut. Available at liquor stores and supermarkets, they are used to make Piña Coladas and other tropical drinks.

> 1 package (8 oz) cream cheese, softened
> 1 teaspoon vanilla extract
> ¾ cup coconut snow
> ¼ cup cream of coconut
> 1 to 2 tablespoons lemon juice
> 2 cups whipping cream
> Fresh fruit for garnish, such as strawberries or kiwi fruit
> Toasted coconut (optional)

1. In large bowl of electric mixer or food processor fitted with steel blade, beat together cream cheese and vanilla.

2. Beat in coconut snow, cream of coconut (stir well before adding), and lemon juice.

3. In another bowl, whip cream until it forms soft peaks. Fold into cream cheese mixture.

4. Divide mixture among 6 to 8 soufflé dishes, dessert cups, stemmed glasses, or charlotte molds. Refrigerate 1 hour or longer.

5. Garnish with fresh fruit, and toasted coconut, if desired.

Serves 6 to 8.

Preparation Time About 10 minutes, before chilling

Timesaver Tip Dessert can be made up to a day ahead.

PETITE LEMON SOUFFLÉS WITH LEMON CURD

A thin layer of lemon curd forms at the bottom of the soufflés as they bake.

> ¼ cup flour
> 1¼ cups sugar
> ¼ teaspoon salt
> 3 large eggs, separated
> 1 cup half-and-half
> Grated rind of 1 lemon
> ⅓ cup freshly squeezed lemon juice

1. Preheat oven to 375° F. Stir together flour, sugar, and salt in a mixing bowl.

2. In a separate bowl, whisk egg yolks to blend; whisk in half-and-half, lemon rind, and lemon juice to blend. Stir in sugar mixture.

3. In a third bowl, beat egg whites until soft peaks form. Stir a spoonful of whites into batter to lighten it; fold in remaining whites.

4. Pour batter into 6 or 8 ungreased soufflé dishes, charlotte molds, or ramekins (¾-cup to 1-cup capacity), filling almost full.

5. Place soufflés in a large baking dish containing about 1 inch of hot water. Bake in oven until soufflés are set and top is browned, 30 to 35 minutes.

Preparation Time 20 minutes before baking

Timesaver Tip Soufflé mixture can be prepared several hours ahead and held in the refrigerator before baking. It can also be prepared up to 1 week ahead and frozen. Pour the mixture into individual dishes as directed above. Wrap, label, and freeze at 0° F up to 1 week. To bake, do not thaw. Remove wrap and bake in preheated oven as directed in step 5, 35 to 40 minutes.

SAUCES AND TOPPINGS

One way to serve an impressive dessert when you just can't take a lot of time is to make a luscious topping for ice cream, pound cake, or sliced fresh fruit. The food processor, the blender, and the microwave oven are particularly helpful in making sauces and toppings.

CRÈME FRAÎCHE

The ½-cup yield of this recipe is enough to top 4 to 6 desserts. For more servings, the recipe can be multiplied—to a yield of as much as 4 cups, if you wish. Try Crème Fraîche with Warm Sauté of Summer Fruit (see page 114) or Warm Sauté of Winter Fruit (see page 115).

> ½ cup whipping cream
> (not ultrapasteurized)
> 1½ teaspoons buttermilk

1. Combine cream and buttermilk in a small jar. Cap jar and shake well to mix.

2. Let mixture stand at room temperature 4 to 8 hours; it will thicken slightly and will thicken more when chilled. Store in the refrigerator.
Makes ½ cup.

Timesaver Tip Crème Fraîche will keep up to 2 weeks in the refrigerator.

CASSIS SAUCE

Excellent with sliced fresh peaches, ice cream, or cake. Frozen fruit is perfectly acceptable for making this sauce.

> 1 pint fresh blackberries or olallieberries, or 1 package (10 to 12 oz) frozen berries, thawed
> 2 tablespoons crème de cassis or blackberry liqueur
> Sugar to taste

1. Place fruit in food processor or blender. Process until smooth.

2. Press puréed fruit through a sieve into a bowl. Discard seeds left in sieve.

3. Stir crème de cassis into sauce. Add sugar to taste, stirring until dissolved.
Makes ¾ to 1 cup.

Preparation Time 10 minutes

Timesaver Tip Recipe can be prepared up to several days ahead and stored, covered, in refrigerator. It also freezes well; use within 4 months.

RASPBERRY SAUCE

This classic dessert sauce has endless applications. In the *nouvelle* style, serve a pool of sauce under an arrangement of fresh fruit, a scoop of sorbet, or a thin slice of a rich chocolate dessert.

> 1 pint fresh raspberries or 1 package (10 or 12 oz) frozen raspberries, thawed
> Sugar to taste
> 2 to 3 teaspoons orange liqueur (optional)

1. Place raspberries in food processor or blender. Process until smooth.

2. Press puréed fruit through a sieve into a bowl. Discard seeds left in sieve.

3. Add sugar to taste, stirring until dissolved. Stir in orange liqueur (if used), adjusting to taste.
Makes ¾ to 1 cup.

Preparation Time About 10 minutes

Timesaver Tip Recipe can be prepared up to several days ahead and stored, covered, in refrigerator. It also freezes well; use within 4 months.

CREAMY TOPPING FOR FRESH FRUIT

This rich sauce is especially good over tart fruit. You can use the food processor, fitted with the steel blade, to make this sauce: Combine all ingredients and process until smooth, about 1 minute, stopping to scrape work bowl once.

> 3 ounces cream cheese, at room temperature
> 2 tablespoons sugar
> ½ cup whipping cream

1. In mixing bowl beat together cream cheese and sugar until thoroughly blended.

2. Slowly beat in whipping cream.
Makes ¾ cup.

Preparation Time About 10 minutes

Timesaver Tip Recipe can be prepared up to 3 days ahead and stored, covered, in refrigerator.

Variation Add orange liqueur, grated orange or lemon rind, or other flavoring to this topping.

LEMON-LIME SAUCE

A light, refreshing sauce to serve with fresh fruit.

> ½ cup plain low-fat yogurt
> 2 to 3 tablespoons sifted confectioners' sugar
> ¼ teaspoon each *finely grated lemon rind and lime rind*
> 2 to 3 teaspoons each *freshly squeezed lemon juice and lime juice*

Stir ingredients together, adjusting quantities to taste. Chill.
Makes about ⅔ cup.

Preparation Time 10 minutes

Timesaver Tip Recipe can be prepared up to 3 days ahead and stored, covered, in refrigerator.

Dessert sauces: Cassis Sauce on sliced papaya, Zabaglione (see page 120) on strawberries, and Lemon-Lime Sauce on melon balls.

ZABAGLIONE

Marsala wine, a dark, sweet wine with a taste reminiscent of burnt sugar, is traditional for this classic dessert. Making zabaglione requires nothing more complicated than patience and a strong arm; the sauce acquires its distinctive frothiness from sustained whisking. Be careful not to let the mixture come to a boil as you cook it. Zabaglione is often served over fresh peaches or berries.

> 4 egg yolks
> 1 egg
> 2 tablespoons sugar
> ¼ cup dry Marsala wine
> 2 teaspoons finely grated lemon rind

1. Beat egg yolks and egg in a mixing bowl on high speed until thick and lemon colored, about 3 minutes.

2. Gradually beat in sugar. Beat in wine and lemon rind.

3. Pour mixture into top of double boiler, or into a bowl set over a pan of simmering water. Water in double boiler should simmer, but not boil, and water should not touch the top pan or bowl. Cook, stirring constantly, until frothy and thickened, about 5 minutes. Serve immediately.

Serves 4 to 6.

Preparation Time About 15 minutes

Timesaver Tip Zabaglione can be prepared up to several hours ahead through step 2, then refrigerated. Complete preparation just before serving.

WHISKEY SAUCE

Dessert sauces are a breeze to make in the microwave. This one is particularly good with Autumn Apple Cake (see page 45).

> 6 tablespoons butter or margarine
> ½ cup sugar
> 1 egg
> 3 tablespoons bourbon

1. Place butter in a 2-cup glass measure or microwave-safe dish. Microwave on 100% power 30 to 45 seconds to melt butter.

2. Stir sugar and egg into butter. Microwave on 50% power until sugar dissolves and sauce thickens (2 to 3 minutes), stirring once during cooking. Cool slightly, then stir in bourbon.

Makes 1 cup.

Preparation Time About 5 minutes

Timesaver Tip Recipe may be made ahead and reheated gently in microwave oven or in a saucepan over low heat.

CARAMEL SAUCE

Rich and sweet, this sauce is excellent with either cake or ice cream.

> ¼ cup butter or margarine
> 1 cup light brown sugar
> ½ cup whipping cream

1. In a 4-cup glass measure or microwave-safe bowl, microwave butter on 100% power 30 to 45 seconds to melt.

2. Stir in brown sugar and cream. Microwave on 100% power 2 to 2½ minutes, stirring once during cooking.

Makes about 1¼ cups.

Preparation Time About 5 minutes

CHOCOLATE MINT SAUCE

Here's a quick and easy sauce for the chocolate fans that takes advantage of the microwave oven.

> 1 package (6½ oz) chocolate-covered mint patties
> ¼ cup whipping cream

Place mint patties and cream in a 4-cup glass measure or bowl. Microwave on 50% power 2 to 3 minutes, stirring once a minute, until sauce is smooth.

Makes about ⅔ cup.

Preparation Time 5 to 8 minutes

CREAMY EGGNOG SAUCE

Enjoy the rich eggy flavor of the holiday favorite at any time of the year. It goes well over tart fruit such as blueberries or raspberries.

> 1 egg
> ¾ cup half-and-half or milk
> 2½ tablespoons sugar
> 1 tablespoon dark rum
> ¼ teaspoon vanilla extract
> Ground nutmeg to taste

1. In a 2-cup measure, beat egg until well blended. Beat in half-and-half and sugar.

2. Microwave on 70% power until thick (3 to 3½ minutes), stirring rapidly with a fork once a minute. Remove from oven and let cool slightly, then stir in rum, vanilla, and nutmeg. Serve warm or cooled.

Makes about ¾ cup.

Preparation Time 5 to 8 minutes

Vanilla Cream Prepare as directed above, increasing vanilla to ½ teaspoon and omitting rum and nutmeg.

ICE CREAMS, SORBETS, AND FROSTY DESSERTS

The flavors of homemade chilled desserts are more intense—see, in particular, the Fresh Fruit Sorbets on page 123—and can be more original than those you purchase. With the help of the freezer and the food processor, you can make a number of these dishes quickly; most of them can be made ahead, since they need to chill before serving.

STRAWBERRY DAIQUIRI ICE

Garnish this speedy dessert with a swizzle stick or a sprig of mint.

> 3 cups sliced fresh straw-
> berries or 1 package (12 oz)
> unsweetened frozen straw-
> berries (do not thaw)
> 2 to 3 tablespoons light rum
> 2 to 3 tablespoons sugar
> 1 tablespoon lime juice

1. If using fresh strawberries, spread in one layer on a baking sheet and freeze, uncovered, until frozen solid.

2. Place frozen berries and remaining ingredients in a food processor or blender. Process until smooth. If your machine struggles to process the fruit, let fruit stand 10 to 15 minutes at room temperature to thaw slightly.

3. Serve immediately or store in freezer until 5 to 15 minutes before serving, then place in refrigerator or on counter to soften enough that it can be scooped.

Serves 4.

Preparation Time About 5 minutes to prepare fruit before freezing and to process ice after freezing

Timesaver Tip Recipe can be prepared up to 2 days ahead and stored in freezer. The rum lowers the freezing point of the ice, which helps it maintain a smooth texture.

The beautiful color of Strawberry Daiquiri Ice is as pleasing as its fresh fruit flavor. The dessert is quick to make because you start with frozen fruit, then let the food processor do the work.

Fresh Fruit Sorbet—here, made with papaya—captures the flavor of the fruit; with the help of the freezer and food processor, it's quick to prepare as well.

COOKIES AND CREAM

It couldn't be simpler—and it's a hit with kids of all ages!

1 pint vanilla ice cream
4 Oreo or Hydrox cookies

1. Soften ice cream 4 to 5 minutes at room temperature.

2. While ice cream softens, coarsely chop cookies with a knife.

3. With a large spoon, fold cookies into softened ice cream. Serve immediately.

Serves 2 to 4.

Preparation Time 5 to 10 minutes

Variation The choices are endless. Coffee and chocolate ice cream work well, as do chocolate chip, peanut butter, molasses, and oatmeal cookies.

GINGER ICE CREAM

In this easy dessert, particularly appropriate after an Oriental meal or stir-fry dinner, the assertive snap of ginger is mellowed by the smoothness of the ice cream.

1 quart vanilla ice cream
½ cup finely diced candied or crystallized ginger
1½ teaspoons fresh ginger juice and pulp (fresh ginger forced through garlic press or finely minced)
Toasted coconut or chopped nuts for garnish (optional)

1. Place ice cream in mixing bowl. Allow to soften slightly. Fold in candied ginger, ginger juice, and pulp.

2. Spoon mixture into freezer carton. Place plastic wrap directly on ice cream, then replace carton cover. Store in freezer for 2 to 4 days to develop flavor.

3. Serve with garnish, if desired.

Serves 6.

Preparation Time 5 to 10 minutes, excluding freezing time

Timesaver Tip Ice cream should be prepared several days in advance to develop flavor.

CINNAMON-PEAR FROSTY

The texture of this dessert is best right after it's made; it does not freeze well. And it's so quick to prepare that even when you're entertaining, you can make it right before serving.

3 cups peeled, coarsely chopped Bartlett pears (use 3 to 4 very ripe pears)
2 tablespoons lemon juice
½ cup low-fat milk
½ teaspoon ground cinnamon, or to taste
Sugar to taste, if necessary

1. Toss pears with lemon juice; spread in one layer on a baking sheet. Freeze, uncovered, until frozen solid.

2. Place frozen pears, milk, and cinnamon in a food processor or blender. Process until smooth. If your machine struggles to process the frozen fruit, let fruit stand 10 to 15 minutes at room temperature to thaw slightly.

3. Add sugar, if necessary (this will depend on the sweetness of the pears). Serve immediately.

Serves 4 to 6.

Preparation Time 10 to 15 minutes to prepare fruit before freezing and to process frosty after freezing

Variation Add 1 teaspoon grated fresh ginger or ground ginger to taste.

FRESH FRUIT SORBET IN SECONDS

Streamline the preparation of sorbets by freezing the fruit first, then purée-ing it in a blender or food processor.

4 cups sliced strawberries or peeled peaches, nectarines, kiwi fruit, bananas, papayas, or mangoes (see Note)
About ½ cup fresh orange juice
Sugar to taste
Pinch of salt
Mint or fresh fruit, for garnish

1. Spread sliced fruit in one layer on a baking sheet. Freeze, uncovered, until frozen solid.

2. Place frozen fruit and orange juice in a food processor or blender. Process until smooth, stopping to scrape work bowl as necessary. If your machine struggles to process the frozen fruit, let fruit stand 10 to 15 minutes at room temperature to thaw slightly. Depending on the size of your blender or food processor, you may have to process fruit in several batches.

3. Add sugar and salt (amount of sugar will depend on the sweetness of the fruit).

Makes 3 to 4 cups (about 6 servings).

Preparation Time About 20 minutes to prepare fruit for freezing and to process sorbet after freezing

Timesaver Tip Sorbets can be made about an hour before serving and held in the freezer. After about an hour, the edges get icy and the mixture must be re-processed.

Note Before freezing, toss peach, nectarine, or banana slices with about 2 tablespoons lemon juice to prevent browning.

COME FOR DESSERT

Make-Your-Own Sundaes

*Gaufrettes and
Curled Vanilla Wafers*

*Specialty Coffees,
Tea, and Liqueurs*

For easy entertaining, invite friends in for dessert. With the excellent ice creams and sherbets available at any supermarket, and some elegant dishes, you can improvise a showy dessert that's easy and quick. Add the delicate, light cookies that are traditional with ice cream, and offer a selection of after-dinner liqueurs, as well as coffee and tea. Make-your-own sundaes are also terrific for a child's birthday party.

SUGGESTED SUNDAE COMBINATIONS

Ice Cream	Topping
Chocolate	Crushed peppermint candies
Butter pecan	Crushed Amaretti or macaroons
Mocha	Amaretto or Frangelico liqueur, topped with a dusting of powdered instant espresso or toasted almonds
Vanilla	Lime juice squeezed on the spot from wedges
	Julienne strips of lemon, lime, or orange rind
	Raisins heated with rum until they have absorbed the liquor
Dark chocolate	Shaved white chocolate (use a vegetable peeler)
Citrus sherbet	Julienne strips of lemon, lime, or orange rind
Any kind	Crushed toffee bars, almond bark, or peanut brittle
	Marmalade or jam thinned with brandy

MAKE-YOUR-OWN SUNDAES

For a dessert as simple as this, you don't need a recipe, just a few ideas. Start with the suggestions given above and go on as your imagination directs.

Offer three or four different flavors of ice cream. It's fun to spend some time at the local ice cream parlor selecting a variety of flavors. Choose the flavors that sound the most interesting, or just pick your favorites, but whatever you get, be sure to include vanilla. You might also want to include Ginger Ice Cream (see page 123), Strawberry Daiquiri Ice (see page 121), or Fresh Fruit Sorbet (see page 123) among your offerings.

Once you've chosen the ice cream, add a generous selection of compatible toppings. A nice touch is to make some yourself; see pages 118–120 for delicious sauces that can be made quickly. Other choices might be ripe fresh fruit in season or thawed frozen fruit, nuts, raisins, chocolate chips, little cinnamon candies, and, of course, whipped cream. The chart above will give you ideas for toppings to use with various flavors of ice cream.

Traditionally, sundaes are served with curled or fan-shaped, thin, mildly flavored cookies, which are available in some supermarkets and in specialty food shops.

Provide good-sized dishes and spoons, and invite your guests to do their own thing!

SPECIALTY COFFEES

For a spirited companion to Make-Your-Own Sundaes, serve Irish coffee, or offer your guests coffee mixed with their choice of liqueur. Provide decaffeinated coffee for those who may wish to avoid caffeine.

For each serving of Irish coffee, first warm a mug or heatproof goblet by filling it with hot water, letting it stand for a few seconds, then pouring it out. Place a spoonful of sugar and a jigger of Irish whiskey in the warmed mug, followed by fresh, hot coffee. Leave enough room at the top for a generous dollop of whipped cream.

Coffee also goes well with brandy and a variety of liqueurs—coffee-flavored liqueur, amaretto, and crème de cacao are old favorites. Top with whipped cream, and sprinkle with grated bittersweet chocolate, grated nutmeg, or ground cinnamon for added zest.

Let guests make their own
sundaes from an assortment
of ice creams and toppings,
and serve cookies as an
accompaniment.

INDEX

Note: Page numbers in italics refer to illustrations separated from recipe text.

A

Amaretto Chocolate Sauce, 7, 112
Appetizers, 18-20
 See also Snacks
 Chutney Pecans, 20
 Dijon Crème, 19
 Fruited Brie, 19
 Hummus, 18-19
 light soups as, 20-27
 Mustard-Dill Sauce for, 20
 Puerto Vallarta Dip, 19
 Skewered Tortellini, 20
 Tiny Potato, *18*, 19
Apple(s), 10
 Autumn Apple Cake, 45, *46*
 -Ginger Crumble, 43
 Pork with Toasted Walnuts and, 70-71
Apricots, 10
Artichokes, 10, 89, *90*, 91
Asparagus, 10, 91

B

Baguette Melts, 35
Baked goods, defrosting and reheating, 40
Baking, 39-63
 in convection oven, 13
 frozen batter technique, 43-49
 make-ahead mixes, 49-52
 in microwave oven, 11, 40-43
 yeast doughs, 54-61
Bananas, 10
 New Orleans, 114-15
Beans
 Garbanzo, Feta, and Tomato Salad, 103
 green, 10, 91
 Hearty Black Bean Soup, 7, 32
 Hummus, 18-19
 Rice and Lentil Pilaf, 74, *75*
 Savory White, 93
Beef
 Eliopulos Stew, 78
 Mexican Shredded Spiced (*Carnitas*), 77
 Mexican Steak, 74
 stock, 20, 24
Beets, 10
Biscuits, 40, 58
Blackberries, 10
Blenders, 15
Blueberries, 10
Breads and rolls, 40, 57
 See also Snacks; Yeast doughs
 Angel Biscuits, 58
 Brioche, *60*, 61
 Corn, 49, 50
 defrosting and reheating, 40
 Garlic Herb, 35
 Homemade Hamburger and Hot Dog Buns, 58
 Old Fashioned Potato Pan Rolls, *55*, 61
 quick, 40, 43, 45
 Raisin Scones, 48
 Whole Wheat Loaves, 59
Broccoli, 10, 91, 92
Broiling. *See* Grilled or broiled foods
Brownie(s), 40, 43
 Berry's, *50*, 51
 Binge, 43
 freezing batter, 43, 45, 48-49
 make-ahead mix, 50-51
 White Chocolate and Macadamia Nut, 48-49

Brussels sprouts, 10, 91
Buckwheat Pancake mix, 52
Bulgur Pilaf, 106
Butter
 Ancho Chile, 75
 Blue Cheese, 76
 Chili, *49*, 50
 Dill, 96
 Green Onion and Cilantro, 76
 Lemon-Parsley, 96
 Lime-Cilantro, 96
 Mustard, 96
 Olive-Walnut, 76
 as sauce substitute, 7, 8, 75-76, *89*, 96
 substitutions, 8
 Sun-Dried Tomato, 75, *76*
Buttermilk Pancakes, 52
Buttermilk substitutions, 8

C

Cabbage, 10, 91
 Hot Slaw, 95
Cake(s), 40
 Autumn Apple, 45, *46*
 Baby, 44, *46*
 Carrot, 41
 freezing batter, 43-47
 Lemon-Scented Pound, *46*, 47
 Sour Cream Coffee, 62-63
 Sour Cream Fudge, 44, *46*
Cake flour substitution, 8
Caramel Sauce, 120
Carrot(s), 10, 91
 Bourbon-Mint, 95
 Cake, 41
 puréed, 92
Casseroles, making ahead, 77
Cassis Sauce, 118, *119*
Cauliflower, 10, 91, 92
Celery, 10
Cheese
 and Chile Soufflé, 84, *85*
 Cheddar and Chili Sauce, 82
 Creamy Herb Pasta Sauce, 80-81
 Crisps, 35
 Fruited Brie, 19
 Garbanzo, Feta, and Tomato Salad, 103
 Salad of Pears, Roquefort, and Walnuts, 100, *105*
 in salads, 101
Cherries, 10
Chicken
 Breasts, Broiled, with Seasoned Butters, 74-76
 Chicken Soup with Lemon and Mint, 28, *29*
 Mendocino Salad, 7, 98-99, *105*
 stock, 20, 24
Chocolate
 Amaretto Chocolate Sauce, 7, 112
 Chip Cookies, 51
 -Coconut Squares, 42
 curls, 111
 desserts, 110-12
 Fudge Frosting, 44
 handling, 111
 Madness, 110
 melting, 111
 Mousse in Minutes, 112
 Orange-Scented Chocolate Sauce, 111
 Presto Pots de Crème, 112, *113*
 Sour Cream Fudge Cake, 44, *46*
 substitutions, 8
 Truffle Cups, *110*, 111
 White Chocolate and Macadamia Nut Brownies, 48-49
 whitening in, 111

Cilantro butters, 76, 96
Cinnamon-Pear Frosty, 123
Clam Soup, Sicilian-Style, 28
Coco-Mac Cookies, 51
Coconut-Chocolate Squares, 42
Coconut-Cream Clouds, 117
Coffee Cake, Sour Cream, 62-63
Coffees, specialty, 124
Convection ovens, 13
Cookies, 52
 See also Brownies
 Brown Bear, *53*, 54
 Chocolate Chip, 51
 Chocolate-Coconut Squares, 42
 Coco-Mac or Coco-Pecan, 51
 freezing before baking, 52
 make-ahead mix, 51
 microwave baking, 40
 Peanut Butter, *53*, 54
 Scottish Butter, *53*, 54
Cookies and Cream, 123
Corn, 10, 89, *90*, 91
Corn Bread, Old-Fashioned, 52
Corn Bread Mix, 49
Cornmeal Pancake mix, 52
Corn Muffins with Chili Butter, *49*, 50
Corn-Pecan Muffins, 48
Crab
 Ginger Crab Soup, 22, *23*
 Lime-Ginger, 68
 Toasted Crab Rolls, 36, *37*
Cranberries, 10
Cream Cheese Hard Sauce, 41
Crème Fraîche, 62, 118

D

Defrosting baked goods, 40
Desserts, 40, 109-24
 See also Brownies; Cakes; Cookies; Fruits
 Apple-Ginger Crumble, 43
 Chocolate Madness, 110
 Cinnamon-Pear Frosty, 123
 Coconut-Cream Clouds, 117
 coffee specialties to accompany, 124
 Cookies and Cream, 123
 frozen, 121-24
 Make-Your-Own Sundaes, 124, *125*
 mousses, 112, 114. *115*
 Presto Pots de Crème, 112, *113*
 sauces for. *See* Dessert sauces
 Truffle Cups, *110*, 111
Dessert sauces, 7, 118-20
 Amaretto Chocolate Sauce, 7, 112
 Caramel Sauce, 120
 Cassis Sauce, 118, *119*
 Chocolate Mint Sauce, 120
 Cream Cheese Hard Sauce, 41
 Creamy Eggnog Sauce, 120
 Creamy Topping for Fresh Fruit, 118
 Crème Fraîche, 118
 Lemon-Honey Crème Fraîche, 62
 Lemon-Lime Sauce, 118, *119*
 microwave cooking, 40
 Orange-Scented Chocolate Sauce, 111
 Raspberry Sauce, *116*, 118
 Whiskey Sauce, 120
 Zabaglione, *119*, 120
Dill Butter, 96
Dips, 18-19
Dressings, 99, 100, 101

E

Easy and Elegant Lemon Mousse, 114, *115*
Eggnog Sauce, 120

Eggplant, 10, 91
Eggplant-Mushroom Sauce, 81
Eggs, substitutions, 8

F

Figs, buying and storing, 10
Fish. *See* Seafood
Flour substitutions, 8
Food processors, 15
 mixing dough in, 54-55, 58
Freezers, 14
Freezing batters, 43-49
Freezing main dishes, 77
Frosting, Fudge, 43
Fruits, 114-17
 See also specific kinds
 buying and storing, 10
 Fresh Fruit Sorbet, 84, *85*, 123
 sauces and toppings for, 7, 62, 111, 118
 Warm Sautés of, 62, *63*, 114, 115

G

Ginger
 Apple-Ginger Crumble, 43
 Crab Soup, 22, *23*
 -Curry Pumpkin Soup, 25
 Ice Cream, 123
 Lime-Ginger Crab, 68
 Rice, 106
Grapefruit, 10
 Vinaigrette, 99
Grapes, 10
Green onion(s), 10
 and Cilantro Butter, 76
Grilled or broiled foods, 7
 Broiled Chicken Breasts with Seasoned Butters, 74-76
 Grilled Veal with Lemon and Herbs, 7, 73
 Lamb with Mint Vinaigrette, *72*, 73
 Mexican Steak, 74
 seasoned butter toppings for, 7, 75-76
 Tomatoes Provençale, 95

H, I, J, K

Homemade Hamburger and Hot Dog Buns, 58
Hot and Sour Soup, 22
Ice, Strawberry Daiquiri, 121
Ice cream
 Cookies and Cream, 123
 Ginger, 123
 Make-Your-Own Sundaes, 124, *125*
Irish coffee, 124
Japanese Clear Soup, 25
Kiwi fruit, 10

L

Lamb with Mint Vinaigrette, *72*, 73
Leafy Salads, 101
Lemon
 -Honey Crème Fraîche, 62
 -Lime Sauce, 118, *119*
 Mousse, Easy and Elegant, 114, *115*
 -Parsley Butter, 96
 Petite Lemon Soufflés with Lemon Curd, 117
 -Scented Pound Cake, *46*, 47
Lentil and Rice Pilaf, 74, 75
Lettuce, 10
Lime-Cilantro Butter, 96
Lime-Ginger Crab, 68

M

Make-Ahead Cheese and Chile Soufflé, 84
Mangoes, 10
Meats, seasoned butter toppings for, 7, 75-76

126

Menus and menu planning
  Come for Dessert, 124
  Dinner for a Winter Night, 84
  getting organized, 7-8
  make-ahead main dishes, 77-84
  main-dish salads, 97
  one-course meals, 6-7
  A Salad Buffet, 104-105
  side-dish salads, 100
  Sleep-In Sunday Brunch, 62-63
  Soup and Sandwich Supper, 36, *37*
  with soups, 17
Microwave ovens, 11-13
  adapting recipes for, 13
  baking and, 40-43
  fish and shellfish in, 66-68
  rising dough in, 55, 57
  vegetables in, 88-91
Milk substitutions, 8
Mint Vinaigrette, 72
Mixers, 14, 55
Mixes, 49-52
Mousse
  Easy and Elegant Lemon Mousse 114, *115*
  in Minutes (mocha or chocolate), 112
Muffins, 40
  Corn, with Chili Butter, *49*, 50
  freezing batter, 43, 45, 48
  Pecan-Corn, 48
Mushrooms, 10
  Eggplant-Mushroom Sauce, 81
  Wild Rice and Mushroom Soup, 21
Mussels Étienne, 68, *69*
Mustard Butter, 96
Mustard-Caper Sauce, 70
Mustard-Dill Sauce, 20
Mustard-Tossed Potatoes, 94

N, O

Nectarines, 10
Noodles, Homemade, 106, *107*
Nutrition, 6, 9
Oil, types of, 100
Oil and vinegar dressings, 99, 100, 101
Okra, 10
Olive-Walnut Butter, 76
Onions, 10, 91
  Green Onion and Cilantro Butter, 76
Orange(s), 10
  -Scented Chocolate Sauce, 111
  and Watercress Salad, 84, *85*

P

Pancakes, 52
Papayas, *85*, *119*, *122*
Parchment cooking, 7, 67
  Citrus-Scented Fillets en Papillote, 7, 66-67
Parsnips, 91, 92
Pasta, 77
  Homemade Spaetzle, 106, *107*
  Melon Seed (Orzo), 106
  Oriental Pasta Salad, 104, *105*
  sauces. *See* Pasta sauces
  Skewered Tortellini Appetizer, 20
  Sopa Seca, *30*, 31
  Tortellini in Broth, 29
Pasta sauces
  Cheddar and Chile, 82
  Creamy Herb, 80
  Eggplant-Mushroom, 81
  Italian Sausage and Tomato, *80*, 81
  Salsa Verde with Tuna, 82-83
  seasoned butter as, 7
  Smoked-Salmon Cream, 80, *83*
  Tomato and Pancetta, 82
Peaches, 10

Pears, 10
  Cinnamon-Pear Frosty, 123
  Salad of Pears, Roquefort, and Walnuts, 100, *105*
  Spicy Pear Soup, 25
  Steamed Pears Nouvelle, *116*, 117
Peas, 10, 91
  Herbed Pea Salad, 100
  Sautéed Snow Peas, 96
Pecans
  Chutney, 20
  Coco-Pecan Cookies, 51
  Pecan-Corn Muffins, 48
Peppers, 10
  JB's Red Pepper Soup, 36, *37*
  Roasted Pepper Salad, *102*, 103
Pilaf
  Bulgur, 106
  Rice and Lentil, 74, *75*
Pita Pizzas, 35
Pita Triangles, 34
Pizza(s), *56*
  Crust, 57
  Pita, 35
Plums, 10
Pork with Apples and Toasted Walnuts, 70-71
Potatoes, 10, 91
  Green Garden Soup, 27
  Mustard-Tossed, 94
  Old Fashioned Potato Pan Rolls, *55*, 61
  Tiny Potato Appetizers, *18*, 19
Pots de Crème, 112, *113*
Pumpkin Soup, 25
Puréed vegetables, 92

R

Raspberries, 10
Raspberry Sauce, *116*, 118
Reheating baked goods, 40
Rhubarb, 10
Rice
  Ginger, 106
  and Lentil Pilaf, 74, *75*
  Pecan, 107
  Wild Rice and Mushroom Soup, 21

S

Salad(s), 97-104
  Bombay Tuna, 99
  Buffet, 104-105
  dressings for, 99, 100, 101
  Garbanzo, Feta, and Tomato, 103
  Herbed Pea, 100
  Laura's Composed, 98
  leafy, ideas for, 101
  main-dish, 97-99
  Mendocino, 7, 98-99, *105*
  Orange and Watercress, 84, *85*
  Oriental Pasta, 104, *105*
  Pears, Roquefort, and Walnuts, 100, *105*
  Roasted Pepper, *102*, 103
  side-dish, 100-104
  Smoked Turkey, 97
  Szechwan Sprout, 103
Salmon
  Creamy Dill, 68
  smoked, toppings for, 19, 20
  Smoked-Salmon Cream Sauce, 80
Sandwiches
  See also Snacks
  Bombay Tuna as filling for, 99
  Raisin Scones for, 48
Sauces, 7
  See also Dessert sauces; Pasta sauces
  Mint Vinaigrette, 73

Mustard-Caper, 70
Mustard-Dill, 20
seasoned butters, 7, 8, 75-76, *89*, 96
Sausage
  Italian Sausage and Tomato Sauce, *80*, 81
  with Peppers, and Onions, 7, 70
Sautéeing, 7, 70, 88
Scallops Charlotte, 73
Scones, Raisin, 48
Seafood
  Citrus-Scented Fillets en Papillote, 7, 66-67
  Creamy Dill Salmon, 68
  Lime-Ginger Crab, 68
  microwave cooking, 66-68
  Mussels Étienne, 68, *69*
  Puerto Vallarta Dip, 19
  Salsa Verde with Tuna, 82-83
  Scallops Charlotte, 73
  seasoned butter toppings for, 7, 75-76
  Sicilian-Style Clam Soup, 28
  Sunday Night Seafood Stew, 7, 32-33
  Toasted Crab Rolls, 36, *37*
Seasoned butter. *See* Butter
Shellfish. *See* Seafood
Sherry Dressing, 100
Side dishes, 100-103, 106-107
Snacks, 34-36
  See also Appetizers; Breads
  Baguette Melts, 35
  Cheese Crisps, 35
  Hot Garlic Toast, 34
  Pita Pizzas, 35
  Toasted Crab Rolls, 36, *37*
  Toasty Pita Triangles, 34
Snow peas, 91
  Sautéed, 96
Sopa Seca, *30*, 31
Sorbets
  Fresh Fruit, 84, *85*, 123
  Papaya, *85*, *122*
Soufflés, 40
  Make-Ahead Cheese and Chile Soufflé, 84
  Petite Lemon Soufflés with Lemon Curd, 117
Soups, light-meal, 20-27
  Ginger Crab, 22, *23*
  Ginger-Curry Pumpkin, 25
  Green Garden, 27
  Hot and Sour, 22
  Japanese Clear, 25
  JB's Red Pepper, 36, *37*
  Puréed Vegetable, 92
  Speedy Spinach, *26*, 27
  Spicy Pear, 25
  stocks for, 20, 24
  Wild Rice and Mushroom, 21
Soups, main-meal, 28-33
  Chicken, with Lemon and Mint, 28, *29*
  Hearty Black Bean, 7, 32
  Sicilian-Style Clam, 28
  Sopa Seca, *30*, 31
  stocks for, 20, 24
  Sunday Night Seafood Stew, 32-33
  Tortellini in Broth, 29
Sour milk substitutions, 8
Spaetzle, Homemade, 106, *107*
Spaghetti squash, 91
Spinach, 10, 91
  Butter-Steamed, 96
  Green Garden Soup, 27
  puréed, 92
  Speedy Spinach Soup, *26*, 27
Spreads, 19
Sprout Salad, Szechwan 103

Squash
  buying and storing, 10
  Grated Zucchini and Yellow, 92
  microwaving, 91
  puréed, 92
Staples, 8, 9
Stir-frying. *See* Sautéing
Strawberries, 10
  Strawberry Daiquiri Ice, 121
Substitutions, 8
Summer squash. *See* Squash
Sundaes, Make-Your-Own, 124, *125*
Swiss Chard, Garlic-Sautéed, 95

T

Tomatoes
  buying and storing, 10
  Garbanzo, Feta, and Tomato Salad, 103
  Italian Sausage and Tomato Sauce, *80*, 81
  Provençale, 95
  Sautéed Cherry Tomatoes, 93
  substitutions, 8
  Sun-Dried Tomato Butter, 75, 76
  Tomato and Pancetta Sauce, 82
Tomato paste or sauce substitutions, 8
Tortellini
  in Broth, 29
  Skewered, as appetizer, 20
Tortillas, as Cheese Crisps, 35
Truffle Cups, *110*, 111
Tuna
  Bombay Tuna Salad, 99
  Laura's Composed Salad, 98
  Puerto Vallarta Dip, 19
  Salsa Verde with, 82-83
Turkey
  Breast of Turkey with Mustard Sauce, 7, 70
  Mendocino Salad, 7, 98-99, *105*
  Smoked Turkey Salad, 97

V

Veal
  Grilled, with Lemon and Herbs, 7, 73
  Ragout, 78, *79*
Vegetables, 88-96
  See also Salads; *specific kinds*
  buying, 10, 88
  cooking methods, 88
  dips or sauces for, 18-20
  microwaving, 88-92
  purées, 92
  seasoned butters for, 7, *89*, 96
  storing, 10
Vegetarian Pilaf, 74, *75*
Vinaigrettes, 99, 101
Vinegars, 100

W, X, Y, Z

Walnuts
  Olive-Walnut Butter, 76
  Pork with Apples and Toasted Walnuts, 70-71
  Salad of Pears, Roquefort, and, 100, *105*
Watercress and Orange Salad, 84, *85*
Watermelon, 10
Whiskey Sauce, 120
Wild Rice and Mushroom Soup, 21
Yeast doughs
  See also Breads and rolls
  freezing, 57
  Pizza Crust, 57
  shortcut techniques, 54-55, 57, 58
Zabaglione, *119*, 120
Zucchini. *See* Squash

U.S. MEASURE AND METRIC MEASURE CONVERSION CHART

	Symbol	When you know:	Multiply by	To find:	Rounded Measures for Quick Reference		
		Formulas for Exact Measures					
Mass (Weight)	oz	ounces	28.35	grams	1 oz		= 30 g
	lb	pounds	0.45	kilograms	4 oz		= 115 g
	g	grams	0.035	ounces	8 oz		= 225 g
	kg	kilograms	2.2	pounds	16 oz	= 1 lb	= 450 g
					32 oz	= 2 lb	= 900 g
					36 oz	= 2¼ lb	= 1,000 g (1 kg)
Volume	tsp	teaspoons	5.0	milliliters	¼ tsp	= 1/24 oz	= 1 ml
	tbsp	tablespoons	15.0	milliliters	½ tsp	= 1/12 oz	= 2 ml
	fl oz	fluid ounces	29.57	milliliters	1 tsp	= 1/6 oz	= 5 ml
	c	cups	0.24	liters	1 tbsp	= ½ oz	= 15 ml
	pt	pints	0.47	liters	1 c	= 8 oz	= 250 ml
	qt	quarts	0.95	liters	2 c (1 pt)	= 16 oz	= 500 ml
	gal	gallons	3.785	liters	4 c (1 qt)	= 32 oz	= 1 l.
	ml	milliters	0.034	fluid ounces	4 qt (1 gal)	= 128 oz	= 3¾ l.
Length	in.	inches	2.54	centimeters	⅜ in.	= 1 cm	
	ft	feet	30.48	centimeters	1 in.	= 2.5 cm	
	yd	yards	0.9144	meters	2 in.	= 5 cm	
	mi	miles	1.609	kilometers	2½ in.	= 6.5 cm	
	km	kilometers	0.621	miles	12 in. (1 ft)	= 30 cm	
	m	meters	1.094	yards	1 yd	= 90 cm	
	cm	centimeters	0.39	inches	100 ft	= 30 m	
					1 mi	= 1.6 km	
Temperature	° F	Fahrenheit	5/9 (after subtracting 32)	Celsius	32° F	= 0° C	
					68 °F	= 20° C	
	° C	Celsius	9/5 (then add 32)	Fahrenheit	212° F	= 100° C	
Area	in.²	square inches	6.452	square centimeters	1 in.²	= 6.5 cm²	
	ft²	square feet	929.0	square centimeters	1 ft²	= 930 cm²	
	yd²	square yards	8,361.0	square centimeters	1 yd²	= 8,360 cm²	
	a	acres	0.4047	hectares	1 a	= 4,050 m²	

Acknowledgments

Calligraphy
Chuck Wertman
San Francisco, CA

Additional Photography
Michael Lamotte, back cover
Laurie Black, Academy photography

Photograph of Danielle Walker by Fischella

Additional Food Styling
Amy Nathan, back cover
Jeff Van Hanswyk, at The Academy

Consultants
Susan Kayman, M.S., R.D.
Piedmont, CA
Greg Patent
Missoula, MT

Editorial Assistance
Don Mosley
Jacqueline Kazarian

Copyediting
Naomi Lucks

Proofreading
Suzanne Sherman

Color Separations
Color Tech Corp.
Redwood City, CA

Special Thanks To:

Catherine W. Berry

Christina Chan

Connie Eng

Carrie McCorkindale

Laura Nakazato

Tobi Walker

Gayle Wilson

Friedmans Microwave Ovens

Quasar Co.
Franklin Park, IL